Public-Private-Partnership (PPP) and Economic Development

Theory and Recent Experiences

Public-Private-Partnership (PPP) and Economic Development

Theory and Recent Experiences

Makarand Upadhyaya
Associate Professor,
Department of Management and Marketing,
College of Business Administration,
University of Bahrain, Bahrain

New Century Publications
New Delhi, India

NEW CENTURY PUBLICATIONS
4800 / 24, Bharat Ram Road,
Ansari Road, Daryaganj,
New Delhi - 110 002 (India)

Tel.: 011-2324 7798, 4358 7398, 4101 7798

E-mail: info@newcenturypublications.com

www.newcenturypublications.com

Editorial Office:
4832/24, Ansari Road, Daryaganj,
New Delhi – 110 002

Tel.: 011-4356 0919

First Published: **2020**

ISBN: **978-81-7708-514-3**

Published by New Century Publications and printed at Milan Enterprises, New Delhi.

Designs: Patch Creative Unit, New Delhi.

PRINTED IN INDIA

About the Book

Public-private-partnership (PPP) is a mode of providing public infrastructure and services by the government in partnership with the private sector. It is a long-term arrangement between government and private sector entities for the provision of public utilities and services. In view of the investments made by private sector entities, there are risk-sharing and performance-linked payments made by the government to the private entities. PPP concessions can either be sustained by user charges collected by the concessionaire or through annuity payments made by the government. In case annuity payments are made, they are typically borne by the government out of the annual budgetary allocations spread over time and are essentially in the nature of deferred budgetary payments.

This book explains and examines comprehensively the role, design, structure, and execution of PPP projects in the course of economic development of a country. It addresses a range of matters associated with PPPs from policy considerations to implementation issues.

The book is spread over 15 chapters which have been organized into 2 parts.

Part I (chapters 1 to 7) is devoted to theoretical issues involved in using PPP as a tool of project financing and hence economic development.

Part II (chapters 8 to 15) explains and examines the role of PPP in various sectors of the Indian economy such as energy sector, transport sector, telecommunications and information technology (IT), urban infrastructure and services, and healthcare services. An appendix, bibliography and index also form part of the book.

The book is meant for a cross-section of readers interested in understanding the design and execution of PPP strategies and projects in the context of development finance.

About the Author

Dr. Makarand Upadhyaya is presently Associate Professor, Department of Management and Marketing, College of Business Administration, University of Bahrain, Bahrain. He earned his Ph.D. from the University of Rajasthan, Jaipur in 2010. Additionally, he holds MBA, PGDPM and PGDCA from Vikram University, Ujjain. He has a combined experience in industry and academics of more than 25 years. Widely travelled around the globe, he received the Faculty Distinguished Scholarship Award in 2007 from the Research Council, India. His areas of research fall in the domains of consumer behaviour and strategic boardroom leadership. He also chairs and has membership of various committees and advisory boards. He is the author of following books: *Marketing Management: Concepts, Theories and Practices*; *Marketing Strategies and Management: A Sectoral Analysis*; and *Media Planning: The Impact of TV Advertisements on Children.*

Dr. Upadhyaya has nearly 80 citations by papers published in several journals internationally. He has been the chairperson and keynote speaker at forums on business strategies and economic growth. He has conducted more than 40 training and development sessions for senior and junior level corporate executives on client relationship, behavioural aspects of overseas market, stress management, interpersonal skills, and team building. He has been a guide and mentor to students pursuing Ph.D. and MBA courses. He was a national level sports player in basketball and cricket.

Contents

Part II: Public-Private-Partnership (PPP) Model in India

Preface

A wave of privatisation and deregulation of economic activities has been sweeping across the world in recent years. There has been a substantial shift from the old paradigm of government monopoly in providing public utilities and services to the new paradigm which encourages private investment and provision of these services within a stable, predictable and commercially viable regulatory framework.

PPP is a mode of providing public services, particularly infrastructure services, by a government in partnership with private sector. It is a long-term arrangement between Government and private sector entity for provision of public utilities and services. In the investments made or management provided by private sector entity, there are risk-sharing as well as performance-linked payments to be paid by government to private entity. PPP concessions can either be sustained by user charges to be collected by the concessionaire or through annuity payments to be made by the government. In case annuity payments are made, they are typically borne by the government out of the annual budgetary allocations spread over time and are essentially in the nature of deferred budgetary payments.

Though the possibility of commercialisation of public services has increased tremendously in the recent past, the role of the public sector in the delivery of services and in regulation will continue to be vital. The future, therefore, suggests the introduction of a new framework for PPP in different forms so that appropriate investments are made in the desired sectors.

The concept of PPP is of recent origin and started with the initiative of the Conservative Government in the United Kingdom under Prime Minister Margaret Thatcher, who actively promoted what is known as Private Finance Initiative (PFI). The idea was to make private contractors meet the cost of constructions awarded to them in return for the public authorities agreeing to rent back the finished projects to provide public services.

This enabled the government to build additional social facilities such as schools, hospitals, reformatories etc., without resorting to additional resources mobilization while the private sector retained gains and savings arising from designs and project management and also received from the government agency regular rents for the facilities.

Though the arrangement seemed to benefit both sides, there were criticisms that the government was just *mortgaging the future* and there were apprehensions that the long-term cost of paying the private sector to run these schemes was more than it would cost the public sector to build them on its own.

The term *public-private-partnership* describes a range of possible relationships among public and private entities in the context of development and other services.

PPP refers to the provision of a public asset and service by a private partner who has been conceded the right (called *concession*) for the purpose over a specified period on the basis of market-determined revenue streams that allow a commercial return on investment. PPP is essentially an arrangement where the private sector participates in the provision of services traditionally provided by the government. It is usually characterized by an agreement charge between the government and the private sector, with the latter undertaking to deliver an agreed service on the payment of a unitary charge by the government, a user by the beneficiaries of the service and/or an upfront capital grant. The arrangement normally involves a whole-lifecycle approach with a predetermined period where the private partner is responsible for both construction and operation. There is also some degree of risk-sharing based on allocation of risks to the party best suited to manage them. The three main objectives which motivate governments to enter into PPPs for development are as under:

1. To attract private capital investment (often to either supplement public resources or release them for other public needs).
2. To increase efficiency and use available resources more effectively.

3. To reform sectors through a reallocation of roles, incentives, and accountability.

A major problem in PPP projects is the appropriate allocation of risk. When infrastructure is provided by the public sector, all the risks are internalised within the government and hence the issue of risk allocation does not arise. Successful design of an infrastructure project involves the appropriate demarcation and allocation of risks to the different stakeholders in the project. Clarity in this allocation is essential to avoid confusion in the financing and implementation of commercialised infrastructure projects as the tendency of each stakeholder is to shift the risk to others.

Good outcomes depend on the accountability framework designed to support the partnership, the strength of which depends broadly on two features. First, the public authority must have a governance framework that ensures effective incentives exist to efficiently manage contracts; and second, the contract must be designed to achieve the desired public goals. To institutionalise good governance many countries have therefore implemented regulatory frameworks that not only support the development of PPPs, but also their implementation, monitoring and evaluation.

PPPs, while bringing in private capital and experience, also involve transfer of valuable public assets as well as foregoing future revenues in the form of concessions. To ensure that such arrangements always enjoy high credibility in the public eye, due diligence, transparency, objectivity and probity of the entire decision making process are all paramount if these arrangements are to succeed and continue for future projects.

The role of public auditors, therefore, becomes critical in assessing whether such arrangements are truly in public interest and are also fair and balanced in sharing of risks as well as rewards. Audit of such entities poses a huge challenge and requires a change in the audit methodology as also the approach of public auditors. The audit while promoting accountability should not discourage private sector involvement, investment and innovative management techniques.

The basic intent of PPP is to encourage the private sector to dedicate its capacity to raise capital and the ability to complete projects on time and to budget for the welfare of the community, without having to compromise the profit motive. At the same time, the public sector would retain its responsibility to provide goods and services to the public at large at affordable rates. This arrangement, indeed, calls for a judicious approach to decision making and underscores the need for a framework that enables the private sector partner to make reasonable returns on investments without diluting the standards and quality of services provided. The key to the success of PPP projects is a balanced and fair sharing of risks and benefits between the partners, and transparency and accountability in all transactions relating to the award and management of the contract.

The international experience has been that PPPs are difficult to implement, especially in an environment of inadequate legislative and judicial institutions. PPPs call for competent institutions which can develop healthy contractual relationships, processes and procedures to develop them efficiently. Lack of well-performing institutions in many countries is reflected in several things such as the protracted length of negotiations between public and private partners, the slowness of reaching closure, the lack of flexibility in risk-sharing and the cancellation of many projects with all the resultant wastes.

The creation of durable and high quality infrastructure is a prerequisite for rapid economic development and requires sustained investment supported well by technological innovation, skilled workforce and excellent project management. For governments alone to bring together all these elements is not always possible. This realization has brought together the public and the private sector in a mutually beneficial relationship in the form of PPPs to execute not only infrastructure projects but also engender innovative strategies for social development.

There could be different types of PPPs but they all will have the following ingredients:

1. Government departments or agencies and bodies and entities under them on the one part and selected private sector parties on the other enter into valid and legal contracts.
2. Partnership between the two is meant to provide long-term public services (and/or goods) of required quality.
3. Public sector, while transferring the responsibility to design, construct and/or operate the project to the private sector, retains the overall responsibility to provide the public service;
4. Private sector brings in the required finance, either fully or substantially, to complete the project and to operate it, with the public sector providing right to revenue, guarantees to financiers or viability gap funding/annuity in appropriate cases.
5. Public sector assigns the right to collect revenues arising from the project to the private sector for a defined period based on demand projections, or pays grants or annuity and/or agrees to share any surplus, subject to a balanced sharing of the risks and gains.
6. Value for money is the basic criterion for the public sector to enter into the arrangement.

PPP implies the coming together of two dominant but divergent sectors of the economy, each with different prescriptions and objectives, for the overall development of the community. PPP have emerged as one of the latest and successful instruments of public finance, and are increasingly adopted by both developed and developing countries for building and rebuilding their infrastructure framework.

PPPs offer a unique and innovative method of involving the private sector in the nation building activity and in accelerating the delivery of public goods and services of high quality through joint enterprises, without spreading the limited available resources too thin.

Public-private-partnership in India is defined as a commercial legal partnership between government and private organisation. The Government of India is promoting public-private-partnership (PPP) as an effective tool for bringing private sector efficiencies in creation of economic and social infrastructure assets and for delivery of quality public services. Traditionally, infrastructure development used to occur through the public sector. However, given the scarcity of public resources, and the need to shift scarce public resources into health and education, efforts have been made to induct private participation in the development of infrastructure. These efforts have met with a fair degree of success.

India has systematically rolled out a PPP programme for the delivery of high-priority public utilities and infrastructure and developed what is perhaps one of the largest PPP programmes in the world.

The Government of India recognizes several types of PPPs, including user-fee based BOT model, performance-based management/maintenance contracts and modified design-build (turnkey) contracts. Today, there are hundreds of PPP projects in various stages of implementation throughout the country. In the face of ambitious and enormous investment in the infrastructure sector in the coming years, the Government of India is actively promoting PPPs in many sectors of the economy.

There has been a huge gap in the demand and supply of essential social and economic infrastructures and services. These infrastructure shortages are key constraint in sustaining and expanding India's economic growth and making it more inclusive for the poor. Given the large resource requirements for investment and the budgetary constraints, Government of India has been encouraging private sector investment and participation in all sectors.

Over the years, a PPP eco-system has developed, and currently it comprises institutions, developers, financiers, equity providers, policies and procedures.

India's infrastructure deficit—whether congested roads and ports, inadequate hospitals or wastewater treatment facilities, and slow trains—is a key factor in constraining economic growth and jobs creation, thereby imposing huge costs on society. Low productivity, poor competitiveness, and high costs are some of the consequences of this deficit.

There is absolutely no time to lose in addressing this deficit with every possible means available to the Government. India will be the world's most populated country before 2030, outgrowing China. Without sustained rapid economic growth and the resulting productive jobs, India will be unable to convert its demographic transition into a demographic dividend. This demographic dividend—a very large working population supporting a relatively small non-working population—has propelled other countries to prosperity and higher incomes. Whether GDP and employment grow rapidly or not, India will have the world's largest working-age population and thereafter the world's largest elderly population. For India to earn its demographic dividend, young Indians must have productive jobs, earn well, accumulate wealth, and save for their old age.

India already represents the largest PPP market in the world as the government has sought to leverage the three roles of PPP infrastructure: (a) generate real efficiency gains through construction management and operational efficiency; (b) bring innovation and creativity by infusing new technology and superior management practices; and (c) help accelerate the closing of the infrastructure deficit by attracting private funding much faster than the years it would take to deploy government funds without breaching fiscal targets.

There is also a pressing need to harness the potentially large supply of global funding for infrastructure. In the developed world, populations are aging, with more savings than ever before in the form of pension, insurance and other institutional funds that are looking for stable, long-term returns that infrastructure investments in India could ideally offer. If India can improve the performance of its PPP markets and attract long-term debt and fixed income products, it can easily take advantage of this sweet spot where savings in the developed world can meet a part of its large need for infrastructure investment.

An adequate supply of high-quality infrastructure and its efficient management and operation over the next few decades can drive rapid economic growth that can generate productive jobs needed to employ the world's largest young labour force. Productively employed, Indian workers can earn, save, and accumulate wealth. There is then every chance that India can indeed become rich before it gets old.

Bahrain
June 2020

Makarand Upadhyaya

Explanation of Select Terms Related to PPP

Annuity: In this type of BOT model, the government harnesses private sector efficiencies through contracts based on availability/performance payments. The granting authority pays the concessionaire annuities on scheduled dates throughout the concession period.

Build-Lease-Transfer (BLT): This type of PPP model involves building a facility, leasing it to the Government and transferring the facility after recovery of investment.

Build-Operate-Transfer (BOT): BOT is a framework where the private entity receives a franchise to finance, design, build and operate a facility (and to charge user fees) for a specified period, after which ownership is transferred back to the public sector. This type of arrangement involves greatest level of private sector participation across a set of different functions and often covering a long period. The risk allocation to the private sector may be significant, including volume and finance risk, and potentially price risk.

Build-Own-Operate-Share-Transfer (BOOST): This is a type of PPP model, in which a concessionaire is authorized to finance, construct, own operate and maintain, share a part of the revenue and transfer the infrastructure facility at the end of the period. The proponent is allowed to recover its total investment, operating and maintenance costs plus a reasonable return thereon by collecting tolls, fees, rentals or other charges from facility users.

Concession Period: The period beginning from the appointed date and ending on the termination date of the concession.

Concessionaire: The private player who signs a concession with the government department to develop a project and/or operate a facility as per the terms and concession of the Concession Agreement.

Contract Period: The length of time measured in years that the terms of a contract agreement are in place.

Financial Closure Year: The year in which private sponsors agree to a legally binding agreement to invest funds or provide services. Closure occurs when there is legally binding commitment of private sponsors to mobilize funding or provide services. The definition of financial or contractual closure varies among types of private participation.

Lease-Develop-Operate-Transfer (LDOT): In this type of PPP arrangement, assets are leased out to the private sector under specific terms, to operate and maintain the asset for the term of the concession period, after which the assets are transferred to the authority.

Management Contract: The private partner takes responsibility for managing specified aspects of the service provision. Ownership and investment typically remain with the public sector, although some rehabilitation responsibilities can be transferred to the private partner.

Operations and Maintenance (Service Contract): The Government bids out the right to deliver a specific service or gives part of the undertaking to the private sector for operations and maintenance of the assets.

Project Capacity: It is the size of a project measured in the units of the capacity type assigned to the project. For example:

1. Number of kilometres is used for road, railway, energy transmission, and telecommunications long-distance carrier projects.
2. Installed megawatts are used for electricity generation projects.
3. Thousands of cubic meters per day is used for water treatment plants.
4. Thousands of installed connections are used for telecommunications network and water or electricity distribution projects.

5. Throughput (thousands of TEU per year) is used for seaport terminals.
6. Population (thousand) is used for electricity and electricity distribution projects when information of installed connections is not available.

Public-Private-Partnership (PPP): PPP means an arrangement between government or statutory entity or government owned entity on one side and a private sector entity on the other, for the provision of public assets and/or related services for public benefit, through investments being made by and/or management undertaken by the private sector entity for a specified period of time, where there is a substantial risk sharing with the private sector and the private sector receives performance linked payments that conform (or are benchmarked) to specified and pre-determined performance standards, measurable by the public entity or its representative.

Abbreviations/Acronyms

AAI	Airports Authority of India
ADB	Asian Development Bank
AERA	Airport Economic Regulatory Authority
AI	Air India
AIBP	Accelerated Irrigation Benefit Programme
AICL	Air India Charters Limited
ALHW	Andaman and Lakshadweep Harbour Works
APDRP	Accelerated Power Development and Reforms Programme
ARWSP	Accelerated Rural Water Supply Programme
ATC	Air Traffic Control
AUWSP	Accelerated Urban Water Supply Programme
BADP	Border Areas Development Programme
BCAS	Bureau of Civil Aviation Security
BEE	Bureau of Energy Efficiency
BG	Broad Gauge
BIAL	Bangalore International Airport Pvt. Ltd.
BIFR	Bureau of Industrial and Financial Reconstruction
BIS	Bureau of Indian Standards
BOO	Build-Own-Operate
BOT	Build-Operate-Transfer
BPO	Business Process Outsourcing
BRDB	Border Roads Development Board
BRGF	Backward Regions Grants Fund
BRPSE	Board for Reconstruction of Public Sector Enterprises
BRTS	Bus Rapid Transport System
BSNL	Bharat Sanchar Nigam Ltd.
CAM	Computer Aided Manufacturing
CBOs	Community-based Organizations
CCI	Competition Commission of India
CCI	Cabinet Committee on Infrastructure
C-DoT	Centre for Development of Telematics

CEA	Central Electricity Authority
CERC	Central Electricity Regulatory Commission
CETP	Common Effluent Treatment Plant
CII	Confederation of Indian Industry
CIN	Corporate Identity Number
CONCOR	Container Corporation of India Ltd.
CPP	Captive Power Plant
CPSE	Central Public Sector Enterprise
CSIR	Council of Scientific and Industrial Research
CSS	Centrally-sponsored Scheme
DBFO	Design-Build-Finance-Operate
DBO	Design-Build-Operate
DFC	Dedicated Freight Corridor
DIAL	Delhi International Airport Pvt. Ltd.
DIPP	Department of Industrial Policy and Promotion
DISCOM	Distribution Company
DIT	Department of Information Technology
DMRC	Delhi Metro Rail Corporation Ltd.
DoNER	Development of North-Eastern Region
DoT	Department of Telecommunications
DSIR	Department of Scientific and Industrial Research
DSLAM	Digital Subscriber Line Access Multiplexed
EBR	Extra-budgetary Resources
ECB	External Commercial Borrowing
EDIs	Entrepreneurship Development Institutes
EIA	Environmental Impact Assessment
EMUs	Electrical Multiple Units
FDI	Foreign Direct Investment
FICCI	Federation of Indian Chambers of Commerce and Industry
FIIs	Foreign Institutional Investors
FIPB	Foreign Investment Promotion Board
GFCF	Gross Fixed Capital Formation
GPS	Global Positioning System
GQ	Golden Quadrilateral

HADP	Hill Area Development Programme
IAY	Indira Awaas Yojana
IDFs	Infrastructure Debt Funds
IDSMT	Integrated Development of Small and Medium Towns
IHSDP	Integrated Housing and Slum Development Programme
IIFCL	India Infrastructure Finance Company Ltd.
IIP	Index of Industrial Production
IIPDF	India Infrastructure Project Development Fund
IIUS	Industrial Infrastructure Upgradation Scheme
IL&FS	Infrastructure Leasing and Financial Services Ltd.
ILS	Instrument Landing System
IREDA	Indian Renewable Energy Development Agency
IREP	Integrated Rural Energy Programme
IT	Information Technology
ITES	IT-enabled services
ITI	Industrial Training Institute
JNPT	Jawaharlal Nehru Port Trust
JV	Joint Venture
JVC	Joint Venture Company
LNG	Liquefied Natural Gas
MCA	Model Concession Agreement
MoRT&H	Ministry of Road Transport and Highways
MRFQ	Model Request for Qualification
MRTS	Mass Rapid Transit System
MSMEs	Micro, Small and Medium Enterprises
MTNL	Mahanagar Telephone Nigam Ltd.
NGOs	Non-government Organizations
NH	National Highways
NHAI	National Highways Authority of India
NHDP	National Highways Development Programme
NIC	National Informatics Centre
NIIF	National Investment and Infrastructure Fund

NRDWP	National Rural Drinking Water Programme
NRHM	National Rural Health Mission
NTPC	National Thermal Power Corporation
NUIF	National Urban Infrastructure Fund
NUTP	National Urban Transport Policy
O&M	Operations and Maintenance
OBA	Output-based Aid
PMG	Project Monitoring Group
PMGSY	Pradhan Mantri Gram Sadak Yojana
PMO	Prime Minister Office
PPP	Public-Private-Partnership
PPPAC	Public-Private-Partnership Appraisal Committee
PSE	Public Sector Enterprise
PSU	Public Sector Undertaking
R&D	Research and Development
RGGVY	Rajiv Gandhi GrameenVidyutikaranYojana
SARDP-NE	Special Accelerated Road Development Programme for the North-East
SERCs	State Electricity Regulatory Commissions
SIDBI	Small Industries Development Bank of India
SISI	Small Industries Service Institutes
SOEs	State-owned Enterprises
SPV	Special Purpose Vehicle
SWM	Solid Waste Management
TRAI	Telecom Regulatory Authority of India
TSC	Total Sanitation Campaign
ULBs	Urban Local Bodies
USO	Universal Service Obligation
UTs	Union Territories
VGF	Viability Gap Funding
WLL	Wireless Local Loop
ZCBs	Zero Coupon Bonds

Part I

Public-Private-Partnership (PPP): Theoretical Settings

1

Meaning and Rationale of PPP

Recent years have witnessed substantial progress from the old paradigm of government monopoly in providing public utilities and services to the new paradigm which also encourages private investment and provision of these services within a stable, predictable and commercially viable regulatory framework.

PPP is a mode of providing public services, particularly infrastructure services, by a government in partnership with private sector. It is a long-term arrangement between Government and private sector entity for provision of public utilities and services. In the investments made or management provided by private sector entity, there is risk sharing as well as performance-linked payments to be paid by government to private entity. PPP concessions can either be sustained by user charges to be collected by the concessionaire or through annuity payments to be made by the government. In case annuity payments are made, they are typically borne by the government out of the annual budgetary allocations spread over time and are essentially in the nature of deferred budgetary payments.

1.1 Commercialisation of Public Utilities and Services

A wave of privatisation and deregulation of economic activities has been sweeping across the world in recent years. These bold new approaches have promoted improvement in efficiency and service quality. Whereas the specific motivations and circumstances vary by countries, and within countries by sectors, there are five factors that are leading economies all over the world to consider enhanced commercialization of public utilities and services.

1. The massive investment requirements—arising from rising economic growth rates—are pushing countries to look for

additional sources of financing against the backdrop of fiscal stringency in most countries.

2. The rising awareness of the importance of efficiency in investment, and delivery in the context of tight fiscal conditions, is leading to rethinking on the ability of government-owned entities to supply infrastructure services in a business like manner.
3. Changes in technology now make it easier to charge for marginal use of public utilities. Such technological changes are making possible the introduction of competition horizontally and unbundling of services vertically.
4. The increasing need for countries to compete in the global marketplace is putting additional pressure on them to provide efficient infrastructure services to their businesses in a cost-effective and competitive manner. Higher infrastructure costs in terms of both price and time delays can make the difference between firms being globally competitive or otherwise.
5. The new dynamism and integration of world capital markets have vastly increased the possibility of raising large funds for infrastructure investment on a commercial basis, whereas earlier it was governments which had better access to resources. In many cases, it is now the private sector which has the capability of sourcing large funds internationally.

While these factors are pushing most countries towards the commercialisation of public services, there is also increasing understanding of the social dimensions of these services in poor countries in particular. The state bears a responsibility to provide access to basic services such as health, education, water supply, sanitation and sewerage.

Moreover, despite the new possibilities of competition mentioned above, most infrastructure services retain very strong monopolistic elements. As such, the state continues to be responsible for providing appropriate regulatory frameworks which assist investors and providers on the one hand and protect consumers from monopolistic exploitation on the other. The commercialisation of infrastructure and also leads to a considerable increase in transaction costs which have to be mitigated through transparent and appropriate regulation.

Though the possibility of commercialisation of public services has increased tremendously in the recent past, the role of the public sector in the delivery of services and in regulation will continue to be vital. The future, therefore, suggests the introduction of a new framework for PPP in different forms so that appropriate investments are made in the desired sectors.

1.2 Origin of PPP Approach

The concept of PPP is of recent origin and started with the initiative of the Conservative Government in the United Kingdom under Prime Minister Margaret Thatcher, who actively promoted what is known as Private Finance Initiative (PFI). The idea was to make private contractors meet the cost of constructions awarded to them in return for the public authorities agreeing to rent back the finished projects to provide public services. This enabled the government to build additional social facilities such as schools, hospitals, reformatories etc., without resorting to additional resources mobilization while the private sector retained gains and savings arising from designs and project management and also received from the government agency regular rents for the facilities. Though the arrangement seemed to benefit both sides, there were criticisms that the government was just *mortgaging the future* and there were apprehensions that the long-term cost of paying the private sector to run these schemes was more than it would cost the public sector to build them on its own.

1.3 Definitional Aspects of PPP

The term *public-private-partnership* describes a range of possible relationships among public and private entities in the context of development and other services.

PPP refers to the provision of a public asset and service by a private partner who has been conceded the right (called *concession*) for the purpose over a specified period on the basis of market-determined revenue streams that allow a commercial return on investment.

PPP is essentially an arrangement where the private sector participates in the provision of services traditionally provided by the government. It is usually characterized by an agreement charge between the government and the private sector, with the latter undertaking to deliver an agreed service on the payment of a unitary charge by the government, a user by the beneficiaries of the service and/or an upfront capital grant. The arrangement normally involves a whole-lifecycle approach with a predetermined period where the private partner is responsible for both construction and operation. There is also some degree of risk-sharing based on allocation of risks to the party best suited to manage them.

PPP definitions abound in the literature on the subject. Some of these are as under:

"Public-private-partnerships are ongoing agreements between government and private sector organizations in which the private organization participates in the decision-making and production of a public good or service that has traditionally been provided by the public sector and in which the private sector shares the risk of that production". [1]

The above definition emphasizes the intimacy of the private party's involvement in the achievement of a specified public policy objective. It stresses partnership-type features such as *ongoing agreements*, *participates in decision-making*, and *shares the risk.*

Another definition [2] stresses three different conditions for an arrangement to be regarded as a PPP:

1. First, the private partners are responsible for financing.
2. Second, multiple tasks (financing, construction, operations) are assigned to the private party or consortium.
3. Third, the private party operates the facility.

This definition focuses on functional aspects of the contract, such as the bundling of financing, construction and operations.

United Nations defines public private partnerships as "innovative methods used by the public sector to contract with the private sector who bring their capital and their ability to deliver projects on time and to budget, while the public sector retains the responsibility to provide these services to the public in a way that benefits the public and delivers economic development and improvement in the quality of life".

According to the UN, PPPs which aim at financing, designing, implementing and operating public sector facilities and services will have three main characteristics, namely,

1. Long-term (sometimes up to 30 years) service provisions.
2. The transfer of risks to the private sector.
3. Different forms of long-term contracts drawn up between legal entities and public authorities.

In a paper titled *Managing Public-Private-Partnership*, the World Bank describes PPPs as "long-term arrangements in which the governments purchases services under a contract either directly or by subsidizing supplies to consumers. In other PPPs, the government bears substantial risks—for example, by guaranteeing revenue or returns, on projects that sell directly to consumers".

According to the PPP Cell of the Department of Economic Affairs, Ministry of Finance, Government of India, "public-private-partnership means an arrangement between a government/statutory entity/government-owned entity on one side and a private-sector entity on the other, for the provision of public assets and/or public services, through investments being made and/or management being undertaken by the private-sector entity, for a specified period of time, where there is well-defined allocation of risk between the private-sector and the public entity and the private entity receives performance-linked payments that conform (or are benchmarked) to specified and predetermined performance standards, measurable by the public entity or its representative".

All the definitions discussed thus far have in common a transactional approach to the idea of partnership. The various parties are expected to deliver in accordance with explicit obligations listed in a contract.

The transactional approach to PPPs can, however, be criticised on the basis that partnerships imply commitments that go beyond any contract. In this thinking, partnerships stress collaboration, where the achievements of the selected public objectives or goals are joint rather than limited to a list of stipulated contractual outputs.

A further corollary of the public governance perspective is that performance should be judged at the level of the partnership, rather than simply at the level of the agency. Asking each individual partner to account for its contribution to the partnership, and whether it is getting *value for money* from these contributions, is highly dangerous—it is like separating out the roots of a plant to see which is contributing most to the health of the plant, with the consequence that the plant is significantly weakened. Once each agency has to account in public for whether it is getting more out of a partnership than it is putting in, the relationships in the partnership are endangered. It is more appropriate that agencies should be held to account for whether the partnership is itself working successfully and whether the agency might do more to contribute to its success.

A deeper sense of partnership is, therefore, achieved where partnerships are regarded as collaborative rather than transactional (limited to the contract), and accountability for the achievement of wider public objectives are joint in relation to external stakeholders.

Broadly speaking, therefore, the various PPP definitions seek to clarify an emerging class of public-sector contracts that involve private parties more intimately in the achievement of specified public goals. While no watertight definitions exist, two features appear relevant to a pragmatic approach:

1. The arrangements need to be significant in scale and involve multiple (bundled) tasks.

2. There should be a well-designed sharing of risk between the relevant public and private parties in the achievement of specified public goals.

It is the second feature that conveys the idea of partnership, at least in a transactional sense, while the first assists in excluding minor contracting-out agreements. While it is accepted that collaborative partnerships represent a valid alternative to purely transactional approaches, it is not precluded from the above definition which allows for both.

In most cases PPPs combine the best of both worlds: the private sector with its resources, management skills and technology and the public sector with its regulatory actions and protection of the public interest.

1.4 What is not a PPP?

The way that a PPP is defined in the literature, it clear that:

1. A PPP is not a simple outsourcing of functions where substantial financial, technical and operational risk is retained by the institution.
2. A PPP is not a donation by a private party for a public good.
3. A PPP is not the privatization or divesture of state assets and/or liabilities.
4. A PPP is not the commercialization of a public function by the creation of a state owned enterprise.
5. A PPP does not constitute borrowing by the state.

1.5 Difference between PPP and Privatization

Although PPP is often used interchangeably with privatization yet the former is different from the latter in significant ways. PPPs present a framework that—while engaging the private sector—acknowledge and structure the role for government in ensuring that social obligations are met and successful sector reforms and public investments achieved.

Privatization involves the sale of shares or ownership in a company or the sale of operating assets or services owned by the public sector. Privatization is most common and more widely accepted in sectors that are not traditionally considered public services, such as manufacturing, construction etc. When privatization occurs in the infrastructure or utilities sectors, it is usually accompanied by sector-specific regulatory arrangements to take account of social and policy concerns related to the sale, and continuing operation of assets used for public services.

Unlike in the case of privatization, PPPs are projects jointly undertaken by governments, public sector bodies and entities with private sector partners to provide infrastructure services of the required/improved quality to the public and consumers at large and involves balanced sharing of the risks and benefits. In PPPs, the private sector invariably brings in the necessary finance to build the projects, undertakes designs and construction as also operation and maintenance, in return for the public sector either transferring its right to collect user charges, levies or tolls or pays compensation in accordance with an agreed pattern by way of viability gap funding, annuity or annual charges, based on certain pre-determined norms and principles.

The main difference between PPP and privatization is that in the former there is no permanent transfer of ownership of the assets to the private partner and moreover, the public sector agency remains accountable for providing services of the required quality. Thus, the responsibility and accountability to deliver the goods and services efficiently remains with the public sector, which is not diluted because of the PPP arrangement. On the other hand, in privatization, not only the ownership is transferred to the private sector, but the accountability is also shifted totally to the purchaser, though the government may set standards and retain price/quality control by establishing appropriate regulatory mechanism, as per the relevant legislation.

Unlike private projects where prices are generally determined competitively and government resources are not involved, PPP infrastructure projects typically involve transfer of public assets, delegation of government authority for recovery of user charges, private control of monopolistic services and sharing of risks and contingent liabilities by the government. Protection of user interests and the need to secure value for public money, as such, demand a more rigorous treatment of these projects.

1.6 Key Characteristics of a Typical PPP

All PPPs incorporate three key characteristics: (a) a contractual agreement defining the roles and responsibilities of the parties, (b) sensible risk-sharing among the public and the private sector partners, and (c) financial rewards to the private party commensurate with the achievement of pre-specified outputs.

Other characteristics of a representative PPP are as under:

1. A strong PPP allocates the tasks, obligations, and risks among the public and private partners in an optimal way. The public partners in a PPP are government entities, including ministries, departments, municipalities, or state-owned enterprises. The private partners can be local or international and may include businesses or investors with technical or financial expertise relevant to the project. Increasingly, PPP may also include non-government organizations (NGOs) and community-based organizations (CBOs) who represent stakeholders directly affected by the project.
2. Effective PPP recognizes that the public and the private sectors each have certain advantages, relative to the other, in performing specific tasks.
3. The contribution of a government to a PPP may take the form of capital for investment (available through tax revenue), a transfer of assets, or other commitments or in-kind contributions that support the partnership. The government also provides social responsibility, environmental awareness, local knowledge, and an ability to mobilize political support.

4. The role of private sector in the partnership is to make use of its expertise in commerce, management, operations, and innovation to run the business efficiently. The private partner may also contribute investment capital depending on the form of contract. The structure of the partnership should be designed to allocate risks to the partners who are best able to manage those risks and thus minimize costs while improving performance.
5. Fixed and operational assets are adequately maintained over the project's lifetime. Asset reverts to the public authority at the end of the concession. The stress on long-term service delivery rather than asset creation.
6. Delivery of superior quality and well-maintained assets that provide pre-defined services with a higher level of accountability.
7. Implementation of the project by an entity, which normally has no public sector equity (or minority shareholding by the public sector).
8. Output-based contracts (rather than input-based) for provision of assets and/or services. In this system, the quality and level of service is specified and standards and specifications are laid down rather than specifying the methodology and means of delivery of services. The private partner may be compensated for provision of assets/services through user charges like road tolls or water fees or through annuity payments by the Government/sponsoring authority.
9. PPP projects may be executed through different financial arrangements:

- Contractual payment (i.e. advance payment, progress payment, final payment, annuities etc.).
- Grant-in-aid (i.e. block grant, capital grant, matching grant, institutional support etc.).
- Annuity or unitary charge which refers to the periodic payment received by the concessionaire for financing construction, operation and maintenance of the project.

Projects such as highways can be taken up on toll as well as annuity basis depending on the revenues they are likely to generate. Projects with real estate component are normally user charge-based as against social sector projects such as education, health, irrigation, water supply, which do not yield sufficient revenues, and hence need to be considered on an annuity basis

1.6.1 Annuity Contracts: In annuity contracts, the private entity is paid regularly from public funds, based on its performance throughout the contract period. In the event of private service provider missing performance targets, there is reduction of payment. Annuity payments create a burden on future budgets for the period of contract which is generally longer. The effect of annuity payments is similar to public borrowings which require debt servicing over a long period. The annuity contracts do transfer some risks, such as construction and maintenance risks, yet they are akin to public sector projects as Government funds are assured through the budgets.

1.6.2 User Charge Based Concessions: In the case of concessions based on user charges, the demand risk is transferred to the concessionaires, thereby exposing them to considerable commercial risk in recovering their capital. Concessions based on user charges lead to mobilization of additional resources.

1.7 Sectors/Activities Amenable to PPP

The sectors/activities that are amenable to PPP include, among others, the following:

1. Construction projects.
2. High value projects which need to be completed on time and within budget.
3. Projects where quality of service is very poor.
4. Power generation and distribution.
5. Water, sanitation and refuse disposal.
6. Hospitals, school buildings and teaching facilities.

7. Railways, roads and air traffic control.
8. Housing, stadiums, prisons.
9. Billing and other information technology systems.
10. Pipelines.

Endnotes

1. Forrer, J. et al., "Public-Private-Partnerships and the Public Accountability Question", *Public Administration Review*, 2010, 70(3), pp. 475-484.
2. De Bettignies, J.E. and T.W. Ross, "Public-Private-Partnerships and the Privatization of Financing: An Incomplete Contracts Approach", *International Journal of Industrial Organization*, 2009, 27(3), pp. 358-368.

2

Objectives, Benefits and Problems of PPP

2.1 Objectives of PPP

The three main objectives which motivate governments to enter into PPPs for development are as under:

1. To attract private capital investment (often to either supplement public resources or release them for other public needs).
2. To increase efficiency and use available resources more effectively.
3. To reform sectors through a reallocation of roles, incentives, and accountability.

The above three objectives are explained below.

2.1.1 Mobilization of Private Capital: Governments face an ever-increasing need to find sufficient financing to develop and maintain infrastructure required to support growing populations. Governments are challenged by the demands of increasing urbanization, the rehabilitation requirements of aging infrastructure, the need to expand networks to new populations, and the goal of reaching previously unserved or underserved areas. Furthermore, infrastructure services are often provided at an operating deficit, which is covered only through subsidies, thus constituting an additional drain on public resources. Combined with most governments' limited financial capacity, these pressures drive a desire to mobilize private sector capital for infrastructure investment. Structured correctly, a PPP may be able to mobilize previously untapped resources from the local, regional, or international private sector which is seeking investment opportunities. The goal of the private sector in entering into a PPP is to profit from its capacity and experience in managing businesses (utilities in particular). The private sector seeks compensation for its services through fees for services rendered, resulting in an appropriate return on capital invested.

2.1.2 Enhanced Efficiency through PPP: The efficient use of scarce public resources is a critical challenge for governments—and one in which many governments fall far short of goals. The reason is that the public sector typically has few or no incentives for efficiency structured into its organization and processes and is thus poorly positioned to efficiently build and operate infrastructure. Injecting such incentives into an entrenched public sector is difficult, though not impossible.

Private sector operators, however, enter into an investment or contracting opportunity with the clear goal of maximizing profits, which are generated, in large part, by increased efficiency in investment and operations. If the PPP is structured to let the operator pursue this goal, the efficiency of the public services will be enhanced. Improving the efficiency of services and operations also increases the chances that those services are economically sustainable and provided at affordable rates—even after satisfying the profit requirements of the private operators.

PPP allows the government to pass operational roles to efficient private sector operators while retaining and improving focus on core public sector responsibilities, such as regulation and supervision. Properly implemented, this approach should result in a lower aggregate cash outlay for the government, and better and cheaper service to the consumer. This should hold true even if the government continues to bear part of the investment or operational cost since cost obligation of the government is likely to be targeted, limited, and structured within a rational overall financing strategy.

2.1.3 PPP as a Catalyst for Sector Reform Agenda: Governments sometimes see PPP as a catalyst to provoke the larger discussion of and commitment to a sector reform agenda, of which PPP is only one component. A key issue is always the restructuring and clarifying of roles within a sector.

Specifically, there is a requirement to re-examine and reallocate the roles of policy makers, regulators, and service providers, particularly to mobilize capital and achieve efficiency. A reform programme that includes PPP provides an opportunity to reconsider the assignment of sector roles to remove any potential conflicts and to consider a private entity as a possible sector participant. Implementing a specific PPP transaction often forces concrete reform steps to support the new allocation of sector roles such as the passage of laws and establishment of separate regulatory bodies. In essence, re-examination of the regulatory and policy arrangements is critical to the success of a PPP project.

At its simplest, therefore, the central objective of any PPP is to achieve public goals using private actors. While it is possible in theory to replicate the advantages of private actors in public organisations through, inter alia, greater decentralisation and enhanced governance arrangements, this will depend very much on the context. Low-income developing countries may, for instance, experience capacity constraints related to public service remuneration structures that prevent the optimal deployment of suitably qualified staff.

2.2 Benefits of PPP Approach

Some benefits of the PPP approach are as under:

1. Availability of private capital and technology.
2. Access to functional and technical efficiency of private entities improvising the lifecycle cost.
3. Transfer of risks of project completion and delivery of agreed outputs to the private entity.
4. Public funds are expended only upon delivery of agreed outcomes.
5. Achievement of economies of scale.

2.3 Requisites for the Success of PPP Projects

To ensure that PPPs are properly prioritised and replicable where useful, appropriate institutional investments are required. Where the expertise to create and evaluate project proposals is absent, viable projects cannot make headway. Frameworks which are able to regulate the preparation and implementation of PPPs should therefore be considered.

Capacity-building exercises are also important to enable the efficient design, implementation and managing of the projects and government support mechanisms. Where community participation is central to the success of a project, means must be created for communities to participate in the process of project development and implementation.

2.3.1 Enabling Environment: It comprises, inter alia, the following:

1. PPPs are a marriage of two functionaries and thus a regulatory actor has to exist to govern the PPP project.
2. Leveraging of private funding to a certain level is needed to ensure that it is sustainable.
3. Capacity building should be ensured by setting up of PPP Cells in governments which have regular workshops on related issues.
4. It is important to have a shelf of bankable projects that could benefit from a PPP approach.
5. Advocacy is essential by having a website with all information and processes on projects.

2.3.2 Enabling Interventions: In addition to the enabling environment, further interventions can be considered which can be used to lower the barrier some projects may face in moving from conception to implementation.

1. Standardised documents are needed to ensure a proper and ongoing understanding of contractual obligations and project requirements.
2. Training tool-kits and handbooks should be prepared to help in the design and development of a project.
3. Project development fund is needed to finance the project development of potential PPP projects. This would include the cost of engaging consultants and transactions advisors. Government is then able to make informed decisions based

on the feasibility reports the fund provides.

4. Viability gap funding could be made available for certain projects which have significant social implications but require a partial subsidy to be viable. This takes the form of grants.
5. Development banks can play a catalytic role in the infrastructure sector by financing bankable infrastructure projects.
6. PPP capacity building can occur through multi-pronged interventions and support mechanisms which include technical assistance programmes from bilateral and multilateral agencies.

2.3.3 Institutional Architecture: Many countries have developed institutional frameworks that generally support the implementation of PPPs to ensure that good projects are selected and properly implemented.

While it is not strictly necessary to have a legal framework to drive PPPs, the emergent best practice is to do so. The scale and complexity of many PPP projects places onerous requirements on public-sector actors to manage the associated risks effectively.

For countries with PPP laws, the institutional framework typically involves the establishment of a central PPP unit with responsibilities for: programme oversight and development, the identification and screening of projects, making recommendations to government for project approval, tracking and reporting on contingent liabilities and securing technical assistance funding for programme implementation.

Most countries that have PPP laws do not have a minister of PPPs. Rather, central PPP units tend to be housed in the ministry of finance (MoF), ministry of planning or the ministry of infrastructure (where most PPP projects will emanate from). Experience tends to show that the MoF location strengthens their authority, as the MoF will ultimately decide on the level of public funding to be allocated to specific projects (if necessary) and the overall level of contingent liabilities which may be incurred by the PPP project. Moreover, a MoF will tend not to have less of a sectoral bias and is most likely to be concerned about fiscal affordability and value for money. It is noteworthy that PPP Cell for infrastructure projects in India is housed in the Department of Economic Affairs, Ministry of Finance, Government of India.

Most countries that have broad PPP programmes also have sectoral PPP units in key infrastructure ministries (transport, energy, water, telecommunications, and health) and, less frequently in education and housing. An important design issue is the role of the sectoral ministry units versus the central PPP unit. For smaller countries with a limited PPP programme of only a few transactions, it may be unrealistic to have sectoral PPP units, but rather locate the programme under one central PPP unit.

Public-private-partnership institutional frameworks typically include an inter-ministerial committee with the following functions:

1. Review/approve project proposals submitted by the sectoral PPP units, after review by the central PPP unit;
2. Make key transaction decisions during the course of project preparation, particularly involving such issues as: level/type of government funding/support, impact on consumer charges, bidder qualification criteria, bid criteria (e.g. lowest PPP payment), bid timetable and impact on existing employees (if relevant);
3. Approve the final bid package before issuance; and
4. Approve the selected winning bidder.

Some countries also require that every proposed PPP project receive legislative approval (federal or state level) before officially launching the tender. However, this tends to be time consuming. It is preferable for the PPP law to delegate this responsibility to the executive branch of government rather than the legislature.

Many PPP legal frameworks also have independent audit agencies. In addition to standard audits of the financial statements of PPP companies, these agencies may also provide an independent assessment of the value-for-money and performance of PPP projects during implementation.

2.3.4 Regulatory Framework: Most countries that have introduced private-sector participation in infrastructure—whether through concessions, build-operate-transfers (BOTs), or PPPs—have also established independent regulatory agencies to supervise the regulations applicable to those sectors. A regulatory agency in an infrastructure sector (transport, energy, telecommunications) will usually have the following responsibilities:

1. **Tariff Regulation:** It involves the approval of periodic tariff adjustments in charges to residential and industrial users. Often, the tariff adjustment methodology is embedded either in individual operator contracts or more generally in sector regulations. Tariff regulation is, from an economic perspective, the most important responsibility of a regulatory authority in an infrastructure sector.
2. **Performance Monitoring:** Regulators often also monitor the performance of operators' vis-à-vis the contracts or sector regulations, and impose penalties for non-compliance.
3. **Dispute Resolution:** Dispute resolution between the government and the private operators. In some countries, this role belongs to the regulatory authority. In other cases, it is delegated to expert panels which are set up specifically to resolve disputes between the parties.

Experience of infrastructure concessions in emerging markets in the 1990s demonstrates that the establishment of professional, independent regulatory agencies and adequate dispute resolution procedures have been the most challenging aspects required to ensure the sustainability of infrastructure PPPs.

According to the World Bank, the success of a PPP project will depend on the following features:

1. Governments need to be able to design projects with a package of risks and incentives that make them attractive to the private sector.
2. Governments need to be able to assess the costs to the

taxpayers, often harder than traditional projects because of the long-term and often uncertain nature of government commitments.

3. Governments need contract management skills to oversee these arrangements over the life of the contracts.
4. Governments need advocacy and overreach skills to build consensus on the role of PPPs and to develop a broad programme across different sectors and levels of governments.

It is evident that before launching any PPP initiative the public authority will be expected to undertake thorough groundwork that will involve clear definition of deliverables, comparator costs, a sound understanding of the legal framework, factors influencing the choice of business model, preliminary demand, cost and revenue projections, scope of force majeure and other game changing situations. In this context, the role of independent consultants in guiding and hand holding public authorities seeking to engage in a PPP becomes critical.

A PPP of large magnitude can have a variety of stakeholders all of them being interlocked in complex web of mutually dependent risk sharing arrangement. It could include the main sponsor PPP usually a consortium of parties constituting an incorporated or unincorporated special purpose vehicle (SPV) as each of these parties may bring in their strengths viz., finance, technological know-how or project management skills and one of them may be a lead partner. Besides the government/public authority there will be other stakeholders like financiers, investment bankers, vendors, transaction advisors, insurers, legal experts and public interest groups.

2.4 Role of Private Sector Partners in PPP Projects

The role of the private sector partners in PPP projects is fiduciary and needs careful appreciation. It must be accepted that the private entrepreneurs come into the PPP arrangements primarily with profit motive, and with a view to pursuing their business prospects, which alone impels them to assume the risks associated with the PPP projects. However, these arrangements involve substantial public interest which both the parties to the arrangements are bound to safeguard, with the public sector partner retaining the accountability to ensure it. This does not mean that they are competing between them, but are to work together as partners and colleagues in the process of national development. In auditing the PPP projects, public auditors must appreciate the respective roles of each partner and focus in audit on the achievement of the end results, and compliance with the established rules and procedures at all stages of the project.

The private sector partners have to bring in not only the required finances and suitable technology for the project, but also have to be innovative in approach. There should be no tendency to *over engineer* the projects and to pad the total capital expenditures. They must also have excellent project management and O&M capability, and must be able to demonstrate their commitment to the partnerships. They must not merely look forward to making profits at any cost, but must be committed to providing sustainable and quality service to the customers. The PPP agreements should essentially yield *value for money* to the government or the public sector partner concerned. The public auditor will always be expected to be mindful of the fact that the private sector partner should equally gain from the improvements and innovations brought about by it.

The somewhat conflicting objectives of the public and private participants in a PPP arrangement should ideally get resolved within the framework of the PPP based on shared risks and rewards and should, therefore, not lead to disputes affecting the provision of services to the public at any time during the operation of the contracts. This is best achieved by establishing clear and transparent norms prior to the establishment of the PPP and by entering into unambiguous and specific contract relationships. There should be built into the contracts an efficient dispute resolution mechanism for resolving disputes which may arise, speedily and without disruption to the service provided.

2.5 Issues/Problems in PPP

A major problem in PPP projects is the appropriate allocation of risk. When infrastructure is provided by the public sector, all the risks are internalised within the government and hence the issue of risk allocation does not arise. Successful design of an infrastructure project involves the appropriate demarcation and allocation of risks to the different stakeholders in the project. Clarity in this allocation is essential to avoid confusion in the financing and implementation of commercialised infrastructure projects as the tendency of each stakeholder is to shift the risk to others.

Good outcomes depend on the accountability framework designed to support the partnership, the strength of which depends broadly on two features. First, the public authority must have a governance framework that ensures effective incentives exist to efficiently manage contracts; and second, the contract must be designed to achieve the desired public goals. To institutionalise good governance, many countries have therefore implemented regulatory frameworks that not only support the development of PPPs, but also their implementation, monitoring and evaluation.

PPPs, while bringing in private capital and experience, also involve transfer of valuable public assets as well as foregoing future revenues in the form of concessions. To ensure that such arrangements always enjoy high credibility in the public eye, due diligence, transparency, objectivity and probity of the entire decision making process are all paramount if these arrangements are to succeed and continue for future projects. The role of public auditors, therefore, becomes critical in assessing whether such arrangements are truly in public interest and are also fair and balanced in sharing of risks as well as rewards. Audit of such entities poses a huge challenge and requires a change in the audit methodology as also the approach of public auditors. The audit while promoting accountability should not discourage private sector involvement, investment and innovative management techniques.

The basic intent of PPP is to encourage the private sector to dedicate its capacity to raise capital and the ability to complete projects on time and to budget for the welfare of the community, without having to compromise the profit motive. At the same time, the public sector would retain its responsibility to provide goods and services to the public at large at affordable rates. This arrangement, indeed, calls for a judicious approach to decision making and underscores the need for a framework that enables the private sector partner to make reasonable returns on investments without diluting the standards and quality of services provided. The key to the success of PPP projects is a balanced and fair sharing of risks and benefits between the partners, and transparency and accountability in all transactions relating to the award and management of the contract.

Private sector participation in infrastructure development is not, however, a simple matter. It requires a framework that can enable the private sector to secure a reasonable return at manageable risk, assure the user of adequate service quality at an affordable cost, and facilitate the Government in procuring value for public money. These conditions are more difficult to fulfil than is commonly realized. Because of multiple stakeholders pursuing conflicting interests, risk mitigation arrangements are usually complex. Inadequate preparatory work in relation to the framework for PPP projects, identification of projects, selection of private participants, preparation of strategic plan and project reports, drafting of contracts and other associated activities will only lead to excessive transaction costs, years of delay in project implementation, inadequate quality, and large contingent liabilities to the government. A project beset with such problems even after completion can get enmeshed in a high cost low demand syndrome.

Entering into a PPP contract does not reduce the responsibilities and the accountability of the public sector agencies and the public servants concerned. On the other hand, it places substantial responsibility on them to see that the arrangement succeeds in safeguarding public interest by managing the PPP economically, efficiently and effectively. It is therefore essential to plan and implement PPPs efficiently and meticulously, and without pitfalls.

The international experience has been that PPPs are difficult to implement, especially in an environment of inadequate legislative and judicial institutions. PPPs call for competent institutions which can develop healthy contractual relationships, processes and procedures to develop them efficiently. Lack of well-performing institutions in many countries is reflected in several things such as the protracted length of negotiations between public and private partners, the slowness of reaching closure, the lack of flexibility in risk-sharing and the cancellation of many projects with all the resultant wastes.

Thus, PPPs should take into account the following:

1. Fair and transparent selection process.
2. Assurance of value for money.
3. Improvement of essential public services, especially for the socially disadvantaged and adequate training for those to be involved in the partnerships.
4. Fair incentives to all parties and fair returns to risk takers, combined with commercial success.
5. Sensible negotiation of disputes that assures continuation of services and prevents collapse of projects and consequent public wastes.
6. Enhanced security in the face of new threats and a general improvement in the safety of services provided under the PPP arrangement.

To sum up, creation of durable and high quality infrastructure is a prerequisite for rapid economic development and requires sustained investment supported well by technological innovation, skilled workforce and excellent project management. For governments alone to bring together all these elements is not always possible. This realization has brought together the public and the private sector in a mutually beneficial relationship in the form of public-private- partnerships (PPPs) to execute not only infrastructure projects but also engender innovative strategies for social development.

PPP projects are meant:

1. To encourage private sector involvement in public infrastructure and related services where value for money for the government could be clearly demonstrated.
2. To encourage innovation in the provision of infrastructure and related service delivery.
3. To encourage rigorous governance over the selection of projects and competition for the award of contracts. - Clearly articulate accountability for outcomes.

To put it more succinctly, PPP projects are aimed to provide *improved* public services by sharing risks in a balanced manner. These are also intended to result in enhanced *value for money* for the public agencies concerned through cost effective designing and technology as well as better project management. These are achieved by following a fair and transparent selection process, fair and reasonable incentives to all stakeholders, assurance of value for money and implementation through long-term contracts. Innovation is the key to the success of PPP projects.

There could be different types of PPPs but they all will have the following ingredients:

1. Government departments or agencies and bodies and entities under them on the one part and selected private sector parties on the other enter into valid and legal contracts.
2. Partnership between the two is meant to provide long-term public services (and/or goods) of required quality.
3. Public sector, while transferring the responsibility to design, construct and/or operate the project to the private sector, retains the overall responsibility to provide the public service;
4. Private sector brings in the required finance, either fully or substantially, to complete the project and to operate it, with the public sector providing right to revenue, guarantees to financiers or viability gap funding/annuity in appropriate cases.

5. Public sector assigns the right to collect revenues arising from the project to the private sector for a defined period based on demand projections, or pays grants or annuity and/or agrees to share any surplus, subject to a balanced sharing of the risks and gains.
6. Value for money is the basic criterion for the public sector to enter into the arrangement.

PPP implies the coming together of two dominant but divergent sectors of the economy, each with different prescriptions and objectives, for the overall development of the community. PPP have emerged as one of the latest and successful instruments of public finance, and are increasingly adopted by both developed and developing countries for building and rebuilding their infrastructure framework.

PPPs offer a unique and innovative method of involving the private sector in the nation building activity and in accelerating the delivery of public goods and services of high quality through joint enterprises, without spreading the limited available resources too thin.

3

Identification of Sectors for PPP

For success, PPP must be built upon a sector identification that provides a realistic assessment of the current sector constraints. The sector identification helps the government to assess the status quo, pinpoint gaps and weaknesses, and develop a sector reform strategy or road map, outlining the tools and activities required for reform. In many cases, reliable or comprehensive data on performance are not available in every area, such as financial or technical areas. In those cases, it may be more efficient to focus on the collection of limited, but key, indicators which provide an overview of the overall performance of the sector.

The sector identification should ideally be performed with the support of a team of local and/or international engineers, lawyers, economists, financial analysts, and policy and transaction specialists. The identification is critical to getting the transaction structure right, so allowing sufficient time for the process is important. Depending on the complexity of the sector, the availability of data, and the consultant procurement process, the sector identification can take from 1 to 2 years. A critical part of the identification is the process of consultations with stakeholders.

As a result of the sector identification, the government is able to determine to what degree an enabling environment exists for PPP and what activities are required in advance of PPP to create such an environment. The identification is important for the following reasons:

1. To understand the strengths and weaknesses of the sector and the most promising areas for efficiency increases.
2. To regularly gauge and report on the progress of reform.
3. To tweak the reform programme as needed.

Ideally, the identification process should cover the following:

1. Technical issues.
2. Legal, regulatory and policy frameworks.
3. Institutional and capacity status.
4. Commercial, financial and economic issues.
5. Consultations with the stakeholders.
6. Realistic sector strategy and roadmap.
7. Government commitment and a designated key person.

3.1 Technical Issues

Government should assess current technical constraints in the sector to be reformed including system efficiency, utility operations, and responsiveness to customers. It should determine the degree to which operational issues are a result of underinvestment, poor investment planning, maintenance, ineffective management, lack of operational expertise, or other issues. Investments underway and investments planned, as well as existing assets, should be catalogued—to the degree that this information is relevant to the reform and can be obtained in a cost-effective manner.

Technical considerations should take into account connectivities, links, and interdependencies of various infrastructure elements (e.g. electricity generation vs. distribution, connectivity of transport modes, validity of tickets/billing across transport modes, technical standards to be followed etc.).

3.2 Legal, Regulatory and Policy Frameworks

The identification should cover the existing legal, regulatory, and policy frameworks including the following:

1. Applicable laws and existing regime for assigning authority and setting performance standards.
2. Oversight arrangements, regulatory bodies, regulations.
3. Major sector institutions and government entities related to the sector.
4. Tariff and subsidy policies and arrangements.
5. Existence and applicability of legally mandated service quality standards.

6. Natural resource safeguards and management requirements important to sector performance.
7. Environmental and health regulations.
8. Relevant labour laws and regulations.
9. Limitations on foreign ownership/sector participation, foreign exchange restrictions, and limitations on repatriation of profits (i.e. foreign investment laws).

The regulatory regime may have to be reformed and/or regulatory bodies created to facilitate a shift from purely government-provided services to the private provision of services. Enabling legal, regulatory, and policy environments are critical to a sustainable PPP. At a baseline level, a legal environment that can support private sector involvement in critical services is needed. The legal environment has to minimize the likelihood of corruption and must be sufficiently reliable as to encourage private participation and investment. To the degree that the legal and judicial environment is not defined, investors and project participants will see the project as unpredictable and highly risky.

Similarly, possible investors must have confidence that the laws and the contract will be respected and can be enforced in the courts or through arbitration, if necessary. The framework for economic regulation must be equally explicit. This may entail creating an independent regulator, a regulatory unit within a part of government, or another form of regulatory capacity. It can also be effective to embed regulatory principles within the contract. Highly specific contract terms that establish duties, performance targets, tariff level and structure, rules for changing tariffs, and dispute resolution procedures, allow the private sector to better predict the profitability of the venture and decide what the contract is worth bidding for. The basic principle is that the level of service demanded and the costs of those services must be equitably balanced, while creating incentives for improved efficiencies in the system.

3.3 Institutional and Capacity Status

PPP requires a range of stakeholders within and outside government to take on new roles or perform existing roles in improved ways. Often, new entities are created—such as PPP regulators—to manage the process. Government must understand the institutional requirements of the reform strategy as, for example, whether the institutional and legislative frameworks are in place to support sector improvement through PPP. These institutional roles must be clarified at the latest by the time the PPP process is complete. However, the greater is the degree of uncertainty about institutional roles during the PPP process, the higher will be the level of perceptive risk for potential investors.

At the same time, there must be some flexibility to refine and update institutional roles as the sector evolves and matures. As decentralization takes roots, governments have the additional burden of determining at what level of government each role is best performed. It is important not to overlook the capacity to support bidding, negotiation, and contract compliance and monitoring. Governments may have unrealistic expectations of the ability of their own organizations in that respect.

3.4 Commercial, Financial and Economic Issues

As part of the identification assessment, the current commercial, financial, and economic arrangements and outcomes of the sector should be understood and assessed. This understanding of the current scenario is necessary to take decisions about the desired sector outcomes and how these might be achieved.

3.4.1 Commercial Considerations: These relate to the business orientation of the infrastructure service provider which may become a partner in the PPP. In preparation to a PPP, preliminary improvements to the billing system, customer database, the status of receivables and funding arrangements may be necessary. These may be needed to improve the financial position of the service provider prior to entering into a PPP.

3.4.2 Financial Considerations: These pertain to the design of detailed and realistic pricing strategies including customer tariffs, off-take agreements etc. The objective is to provide affordable services, while providing the private partner with revenue sufficient for commercially viable operations. Sometimes, the government's provision of financial support through investment contributions—or other forms of *viability gap* support or even ongoing subsidies—can achieve this balance.

In short, financial model needs to be developed to review available data, identify key points of sensitivity, and continually update critical assumptions and results through ongoing review as the transaction develops.

The first step in financial analysis and modelling is the collection and analysis of historical data, including financial, organizational, operational and technical information. Data required would include, inter alia, the following:

1. Audited financial statements.
2. Tariff schedules—historical and current.
3. Employees—numbers and types.
4. Database of customers.
5. Debt schedule and cost of capital.
6. Schedule of operating assets.
7. Details of any ongoing and planned capital investment programmes.

In addition to sector-specific data, gathering critical macroeconomic information (e.g. inflation rate and exchange rate) is important. Similarly, demographic information (population growth, degree of urbanization, sex ratio etc.) is also crucial. These macroeconomic and demographic data are needed to project such key elements as demand, required tariff adjustments, operating costs, revenues, investments, and debt service.

3.4.3 Economic Considerations: These relate to the overall cost/benefit analysis of the proposed PPP and its projected impact on the sector. While this analysis begins in the identification stage, it continues throughout the PPP process as an iterative analysis of the PPP structure as it evolves.

There should be analysis of the financial flows within the sector, the financing gaps, and the commercial results. Where the sector is falling short of government and consumer expectations, an agreement should be reached to establish realistic financial expectations of stakeholders.

3.5 Consultations with Stakeholders

PPPs are generally controversial. This is partly due to the diverse range of stakeholders involved in the process and the difficulty in reconciling their interests and concerns. In addition, too often the stakeholders are not properly consulted or engaged in the process. Consultation is increasingly seen as important for several reasons:

1. Inadequate consultation or communication with stakeholders increases the risk of opposition, often late in the process, leading to delays or even cancellation.
2. Stakeholders provide valuable inputs to the design and practicality of the project. Permitting stakeholders to comment on PPP strategies allows for a sense of buy-in and can lead to innovative approaches.
3. Broad public support and understanding of the reform agenda encourage politicians to stay committed.
4. Dissemination of information leads to increased credibility of project partners.

Consultation is a less formal process through which themes and policies of interest are discussed within or across stakeholder groups. It is intended to gather information and build an understanding among the reformers as to current perceptions and understanding and the basis of those opinions. A key part of stakeholder consultation is to manage expectations with respect to how feedback will be incorporated into the reform process, i.e. the feedback may not translate into direct change in the PPP design or process but will be one stream of influence. This might be accomplished through focus groups or stakeholder discussion groups.

In spite of these compelling reasons, some governments see risk in public consultations because of the danger of raising expectations that may not be met. Likewise, consultations may fuel opposition. These risks are easily outweighed by the benefits of communication and the crucial role it plays in building support for, and understanding of, PPP. There must be a consultation process to reconcile and prioritize issues, leading to broad agreement on the objectives of PPP.

For stakeholders to play an active role in the PPP process, they must be given not only a forum for participation but also the information they need to participate effectively. The appropriate forum to communicate and build support for PPP is through an iterative dialogue with stakeholders. Each communications programme must be tailored to the local context and PPP, but should include some or all the components explained below.

3.5.1 Public Awareness and Education: Public awareness efforts are aimed at a broad range of stakeholders and designed to increase general awareness of an issue. This is a proactive distribution of information that will help inform public reaction to PPP. This might be done through TV, radio, town meetings, and newspapers.

Public education is the process of providing stakeholders with the tools and information required to increase understanding of an issue or to take on a new role. This is a more specific and detailed programme than public awareness.

Communication activities have to begin early in the process and continue through to closure and even during implementation. The project structure should incorporate mechanisms to ensure ongoing communication with the public and customers. The communication programme associated with PPP has to occur not only at all stages of PPP, but on several levels—at the level of decision-makers, among the stakeholders specifically affected by a PPP, and among the public at large as needed.

3.5.2 Opinion Research: Furthermore, there is need for

opinion research, i.e. gathers data on stakeholders, their perceptions, and behaviours with respect to the issues concerning a specific PPP. The research influences the content and media of the communications programme as well as the reforms themselves. The research is conducted on a relatively formal basis through questionnaires, polling, etc.

3.6 Realistic Sector Strategy and Road Map

The identification assessment of the sector yields information to develop targeted, specific, and realistic sector strategy and road map to achieve improvements, through PPPs and other interventions. The strategy and road map provide clarity and certainty about the operating environment to private sector operators—a prerequisite for sizable investments and long payback periods inherent in infrastructure projects. Sector strategies may rely on breaking down service functions, e.g. between power generation and distribution—resulting in complex linkages that need to be defined before a PPP can realistically be implemented.

The road map provides the context, sets out sector goals, and describes the steps to be taken to prepare for and implement PPP. A well-defined road map and a well-managed process provide a degree of certainty and reassurance to all participants. The road map and PPP process should incorporate a timetable that should be adhered to as closely as possible. Decision-makers and participants must be made aware of key dates and milestones. The road map and the activities it encompasses must be subject to continual updating. As the transaction evolves and is further defined, the specific requirements for implementation become clearer and required activities can be outlined in detail.

3.7 Government Commitment and a Designated Key Person

The private sector will expect government to be a competent partner in discharging its obligations in terms of policy and reform planning, project development, and contract oversight. It will also expect that the government has established the appropriate legal and other frameworks to set targets; monitor, evaluate, and report progress; enforce the contract provisions, and handle disputes. A detailed roadmap helps manage expectations in that regard, and allows the actual performance of the government to be monitored and measured.

The commitment of government to the strategy is demonstrated in several ways, particularly through: (a) a public statement of the reform strategy and expectations of PPP, (b) stakeholder consultations and transparency of process, (c) the provision of adequate funding and support for the process and (d) the appointment of a powerful key person for the process.

The key person is an individual who is accountable for progress of the project. He/she is a focal point for public communication and information, and ensures that appropriate attention is given to the main issues. He/she works with various parties to achieve co-operation/consensus and leads the government toward decisions. The standing, credibility, and strength of mandate of the PPP key person are strong indications of the true commitment of the government to the PPP project.

Political changes and powerful vested interests can all constrain the PPP process. The government has to set out the case for PPP in a convincing and transparent manner, anticipating concerns and questions. In this way, broader support for PPP can be earned, and short-term political pressures can be faced successfully. However, popular support for PPPs is ultimately gained through results—in terms of improved services and reasonable costs.

4

Types and Formats of PPP Contracts

PPP is one tool available to decision makers in reforming infrastructure or service delivery. It is most effective when it is accompanied by other reform activities to underpin and reinforce the PPP and to support sustainable improvement. A successful PPP is designed with careful attention to the context or the enabling environment within which the partnership will be implemented. Where the operating environment can be reformed to be more conducive to the goals of PPP, this should be accomplished. Where elements of the operating context cannot be changed, the PPP design must be tailored to accommodate existing conditions.

Therefore, in designing a PPP process and selecting a form of PPP, it is important to consider the following factors:

1. Objectives of the reform.
2. Policy environment.
3. Legal, regulatory, and institutional frameworks.
4. Financing requirements and resources of the sector.
5. Political constraints and stakeholder concerns.

PPP will be an effective tool to address some, but probably not all, sector issues.

Various types of PPP options are available for consideration. Each option presents different characteristics to be assessed against the sector reform objectives. Further, each PPP option implies varying levels of responsibility and risk to be assumed by the private operator, together with differences in structures and contract forms. Increasingly, contracts are becoming hybrids, adopting features of several contracts to reflect the best local requirements.

The basic PPP contract types are as under:

1. Service contracts.

2. Management contracts.
3. Lease contracts or affermage.
4. Concessions.
5. Build-operate-transfer (BOT).
6. Joint ventures.
7. Hybrid arrangements.

Following paragraphs provide an overview of the key features of each option as well as some inherent advantages and disadvantages. In addition, decision-makers should consider carefully the local capacity available to implement options that are more complex. PPPs with complicated financial structures and/or extensive contractual or monitoring requirements will necessitate hiring and/or training staff, a process that has to be accomplished in advance of the need.

Finally, it should be noted that different PPP forms are more readily adapted to particular sectors or project types and have been used more extensively in these contexts. As part of the selection process, decision-makers should note the prior depth of experience in using a particular type of PPP in a particular sector.

4.1 Service Contracts

Under a service contract, the government (public authority) hires a private company or entity to carry out one or more specified tasks or services for a period, typically 1 to 3 years. The public authority remains the primary provider of the infrastructure service and contracts out only portions of its operation to the private partner. The private partner must perform the service at the agreed cost and must typically meet performance standards set by the public sector. Governments generally use competitive bidding procedures to award service contracts, which tend to work well given the limited period and narrowly defined nature of these contracts.

Under a service contract, the government pays the private partner a pre-determined fee for the service, which may be based on a one-time fee, unit cost, or other basis. Therefore, the profit of contractor increases if he can reduce his operating costs, while meeting required service standards. One financing option involves a cost-plus-fee formula, where costs such as labour are fixed, and the private partner participates in a profit-sharing system. The private partner typically does not interact with the consumers. The government is responsible for funding any capital investments required to expand or improve the system.

4.1.1 Advantages: Service contracts are usually most suitable where the service can be clearly defined in the contract, the level of demand is reasonably certain, and performance can be monitored easily. Service contracts provide a relatively low-risk option for expanding the role of the private sector. Service contracts can have a quick and substantial impact on system operation and efficiency, and provide a vehicle for technology transfer and development of managerial capacity.

Service contracts are often short-term, allowing for repeated competition in the sector. The barriers to entry are also low given that only a discrete service is up for bid. The repeated bidding maintains pressure on contractors to maintain low costs, while the low barriers to entry encourage participation in the competition.

4.1.2 Disadvantages: Service contracts are unsuitable if the main objective is to attract capital investment. The contracts may improve efficiency and thus release some revenue for other purposes, but the contractor is not under an obligation to provide financing. The effectiveness of the contractor may actually be compromised if other sources of financing (e.g. government or donors) do not materialize. The fact that the activities of contractor are discrete and segregated from the broader operations of the company may mean that there is no broader or deeper impact on the system operations, only discrete and limited improvements. The public sector remains in charge of tariff setting and assets, both of which are politically vulnerable and critical to sustain the system.

4.2 Management Contracts

A management contract expands the services to be contracted out to include some or all of the management and operation of the public service (hospital, port authority etc.). Although ultimate obligation for service provision remains in the public sector, daily management control and authority is assigned to the private partner or contractor. In most cases, the private partner provides working capital but no financing for investment. The private contractor is paid a pre-determined rate for labour and other anticipated operating costs. To provide an incentive for performance improvement, the contractor is paid an additional amount for achieving pre-specified targets. Alternatively, the management contractor can be paid a share of profits. The public sector retains the obligation for major capital investment, particularly those related to expand or substantially improve the system. The contract can specify discrete activities to be funded by the private sector. The private partner interacts with the customers, and the public sector is responsible for setting tariffs.

4.2.1 Advantages: The main advantage of this option is that many operational gains that result from private sector management can be made without transferring the assets to the private sector. The contracts are less difficult to develop than others and can be less controversial. The contracts are also relatively low cost as fewer staff is dispatched to the utility from the private operator. Management contracts can also be seen as interim arrangements, allowing for modest improvements while more comprehensive contracts and structures are developed. Similarly, a management contract can be structured to phase-in increasingly extensive involvement of the private sector over time and as progress is demonstrated.

4.2.2 Disadvantages: The split between the obligation for service and management, on the one hand, and financing and expansion planning, on the other, is a tricky one. There is a risk that the management contractor does not enjoy the autonomy or the authority (e.g. over employees) required to achieve deep and lasting change. If the operator is paid a portion of profits or given an incentive payment, safeguards are required to prevent inflation of reported achievements or deficient maintenance of the system to increase profits.

4.3 Lease Contracts or Affermage

Under a lease contract, the private partner is responsible for the service in its entirety and undertakes obligations relating to quality and service standards. Except for new and replacement investments, which remain the responsibility of the public authority, the operator provides the service at his expense and risk. The duration of the leasing contract is typically for 10 years and may be renewed for up to 20 years. Responsibility for service provision is transferred from the public sector to the private sector and the financial risk for operation and maintenance is borne entirely by the private sector operator. In particular, the operator is responsible for losses and for unpaid debts of consumers. Leases do not involve any sale of assets to the private sector.

Under this arrangement, the initial establishment of the system is financed by the public authority and contracted to a private company for operation and maintenance. Part of the tariff is transferred to the public authority to service loans raised to finance extensions of the system.

An affermage is similar, but not identical, to a lease contract. Unlike a lease where the private sector retains revenue collected from customers and makes a specified lease payment to the contracting authority, an affermage allows the private sector to collect revenue from the customers, pays the contracting authority an affermage fee, and retains the remaining revenue. The affermage can be more appealing to the private partner as it reduces some risks associated with low-cost recovery in sales. The affermage fee is typically an agreed rate per every unit sold.

4.3.1 Advantages: Under lease and affermage contracts,

profits of private partner depend on the sales and costs of the utility. The key advantage of this option is that it provides incentives for the operator to achieve higher levels of efficiency and higher sales. The principal drawback is the risk of management reducing the level of maintenance on long-lived assets, particularly in the later years of the contract, in order to increase profits. Further, the private partner provides a fee to cover the cost of using the assets although the private partner does not provide investment capital.

4.3.2 Disadvantages: The key issue in moving from service and management contracts to a lease is that the revenues of contractor are derived from customer payments, and hence the question of tariff levels becomes increasingly sensitive. This may require structuring and revising complex tariff arrangements. In addition, the responsibility for capital investment remains with the government and no private investment capital is mobilized.

4.4 Concessions

A concession makes the private sector operator (called concessionaire) responsible for the full delivery of services in a specified area, including operation, maintenance, collection, management, and construction and rehabilitation of the system. Importantly, the operator is now responsible for all capital investment. Although the private sector operator is responsible for providing the assets, yet such assets are publicly owned even during the concession period. The public sector is responsible for establishing performance standards and ensuring that the concessionaire meets them. In essence, the role of public sector shifts from being the service provider to regulating the price and quality of service.

The concessionaire collects the tariff directly from the system users. The tariff is typically established by the concession contract, which also includes provisions on how it may be changed over time. In rare cases, the government may choose to provide financing support to help the concessionaire fund its capital expenditure. The concessionaire is responsible for any capital investment required to build, upgrade, or expand the system, and for financing those investments out of its resources and from the tariffs paid by the system users. The concessionaire is also responsible for working capital.

A concession contract is typically valid for 25-30 years so that the operator has sufficient time to recover the capital invested and earn an appropriate return over the life of the concession. The public authority may contribute to the capital investment cost if necessary. This can be an investment *subsidy* (viability gap financing) to achieve commercial viability of the concession. Alternatively, the government can be compensated for its contribution by receiving a commensurate part of the tariff collected.

4.4.1 Advantages: Concessions are an effective way to attract private finance required to fund new construction or rehabilitate existing facilities. A key advantage of the concession arrangement is that it provides incentives to the operator to achieve improved levels of efficiency and effectiveness since gains in efficiency translate into increased profits and return to the concessionaire. The transfer of the full package of operating and financing responsibilities enables the concessionaire to prioritize and innovate as it deems most effective.

4.4.2 Disadvantages: Main drawbacks of this option include the complexity of the contract required to define the operator's activities. Governments also need to upgrade their regulatory capacity in relation to tariffs and performance monitoring. Further, the long-term of the contracts complicates the bidding process and contract design, given the difficulty in anticipating events over a 25-year period. This drawback may be countered by allowing a periodic review of certain contract terms in the context of the evolving environment. There is additional risk that the operator will only invest in new assets where it expects payback within the remaining period of the contract unless provisions for these events are set out in the contract. Moreover, due to the long-term and comprehensive nature of the contracts, they can be politically controversial and difficult to organize. It is argued that concessions provide only limited competition given the limited number of qualified operators for a major infrastructure network.

4.5 Build-Operate-Transfer (BOT)

Of late, different countries have adopted various methods for attracting private sector funds for infrastructure development. The most prominent, and possibly the most widely used, is the build-operate-transfer (BOT) arrangement. As the term suggests, the private investor (concessionaire) builds, operates and transfers the facility back to the government at the end of a specified period, called the concession period. A transparent regulatory framework is needed to make BOT type projects easier to negotiate and implement.

BOT and similar arrangements are a kind of specialized concession in which a private firm or consortium finances and develops a new infrastructure project or a major component according to performance standards set by the government.

Under BOT, the private partner provides the capital required to build the new facility. Importantly, the private operator now owns the assets for a period set by the contract—sufficient to allow the developer time to recover investment costs through user charges. The public sector agrees to purchase a minimum level of output produced by the facility, sufficient to allow the operator to recover its costs during operation. A difficulty emerges if the public sector has over-estimated demand and finds itself purchasing output under such an agreement (*take-or-pay*) when the demand does not exist. Alternatively, the distribution utility might pay a capacity charge and a consumption charge, thus sharing the demand risk between the public and private partners. BOT generally requires complicated financing packages to achieve the large financing amounts and long repayment periods required. At the end of the contract, the public sector assumes ownership but can opt to assume operating responsibility, contract the operation responsibility to the developer, or award a new contract to a new partner.

The distinction between a BOT-type arrangement and a concession is that a concession generally involves extensions to and operation of existing systems, whereas a BOT generally involves large *green field* investments requiring substantial outside finance, for both equity and debt. However, in practice, a concession contract may include the development of major new components as well as extensions to existing systems, and BOT sometimes involves expansion of existing facilities.

There are many variations of the basic BOT structure including build-transfer-operate (BTO) where the transfer to the public owner takes place at the conclusion of construction rather than the end of the contract. Under build-own-operate (BOO) the developer constructs and operates the facility without transferring ownership to the public sector. Under a design-build-operate (DBO) contract, ownership is never in private hands. Instead, a single contract is let out for design, construction, and operation of the infrastructure project.

The questions of ownership and the timing of the transfer are generally determined by local law and financing conditions, and the number of possible permutations is large.

Under the design-build-finance-operate (DBFO) approach, the responsibilities for designing, building, financing, and operating are bundled together and transferred to private sector partners. DBFO arrangements vary greatly in terms of the degree of financial responsibility that is transferred to the private partner.

4.5.1 Advantages: BOT arrangements have been widely used to attract private financing to the construction or renovation of infrastructure. BOT agreements tend to reduce commercial risk for the private partner because there is often only one customer, the government. However, the private partner must be confident that the purchase agreement will be honoured.

The advantage of DBFO projects is that they are financed partly or completely by debt, which leverages revenue streams dedicated to the project. Direct user fees (like tolls) are the most common revenue source. However, other sources of finance in the road sector, for instance, might include lease payments, shadow tolls, and vehicle registration fees.

4.5.2 Disadvantages: BOT agreements have a project-specific application so they are potentially a good vehicle for a specific investment, but with less impact on overall system performance. It can be difficult to link the increases in production brought about by a BOT with commensurate improvements on the demand side. While initial capital construction costs may be reduced through the private sector's experience, private debt may be an expensive substitute for public financing where a *take-or-pay* agreement is in place. The benefit of competition is limited to the initial bidding process and these contracts are often renegotiated during their life. The tender documents and processes require careful design and adequate time.

4.6 Joint Ventures

Joint ventures are alternatives to full privatization in which the infrastructure is co-owned and operated by the public sector and private operators. Under a joint venture, the public and private sector partners can either form a new company or assume joint ownership of an existing company through a sale of shares to one or several private investors. The company may also be listed on the stock exchange. A key requirement of this structure is good corporate governance, in particular the ability of the company to maintain independence from the government. This is important because the government is both part owner and regulator, and officials may be tempted to meddle in the company's business to achieve political goals. From its position as shareholder, however, the government has an interest in the profitability and sustainability of the company and can work to smooth political hurdles. The private partner assumes the operational role and a board of directors generally reflects the shareholding composition or expert representation.

The joint venture structure is often accompanied by additional contracts (concessions or performance agreements) that specify the expectations of the company. Joint ventures also take some time to develop and allow the public and private partners considerable opportunity for dialogue and cooperation before the project is implemented. Under the joint venture structure, both public and private partners have to be willing to invest in the company and share certain risks.

4.6.1 Advantages: Joint ventures are real partnerships of the public and private sectors that match the advantages of the private sector with the social concerns and local knowledge of the public sector. Under a joint venture, all partners invest in the company and have an interest in the success of the company and incentives for efficiency.

4.6.2 Disadvantages: Government's dual roles as owner and regulator can lead to conflict of interest. Joint ventures also have a tendency to be directly negotiated or to follow a less formal procurement path, which can lead to concern for corruption.

4.7 Hybrid Arrangements

Contract arrangements that incorporate different characteristics of a range of contract types can also be developed. Called *hybrid arrangements*, these bring together the attributes most suitable to a particular project's requirements and the operating conditions. Hybrid arrangements provide a tailored solution in terms of scope, risk sharing, and/or scope that is most directly suitable to the project at hand. Obviously, the variations are endless.

Thus, a *management contract plus* arrangement is one under which the performance-related element of the management contract is substantial enough to transfer real risk. For instance, the payment of bonuses to the management contractor might be linked to achievement to increases in the operating cash flow of the utility by a pre-determined amount. To achieve the bonus, the contractor may put additional inputs at risk to achieve the cash flow outputs.

Similarly, an *affermage-lease plus* arrangement has the ability to share responsibility for investments. Under a standard affermage/lease, the contracting authority retains full responsibility for undertaking and financing new investment even though the operator may be in a better position to manage new construction and some other investment obligations.

In some cases, the operator is given a limited investment responsibility, such as extension of network service coverage in certain areas. Alternatively, the operator and contracting authority may reach an agreement to co-finance investments.

All the PPP models described above may not be absolutely distinct from one another. In fact different PPP models may have overlapping features. What, however, distinguishes each type of PPP model from one another is the degree of risk and responsibility borne by the private sector partner.

4.8 Selecting the Appropriate Option

PPP should be implemented within an overall reform strategy. The objectives of a PPP project should be a sub-set of the objectives for the overall sector reform. Selecting an appropriate PPP option is based on the following factors:

1. PPP options available.
2. Technical constraints and goals of the sector.
3. Legal and regulatory constraints.
4. Institutional issues.
5. Commercial, financial, and financing requirements and constraints.
6. Interest of the market (local and international).
7. Special requirements of the sector based on characteristics of the system/population.

Selecting a PPP option is influenced by the specific objectives of the government. Reform objectives should be compared with the results of the identification and features of each contract type, its advantages and disadvantages, likely outcomes and prerequisites. From this analysis, it should be possible to determine which option is most likely to succeed at meeting the greatest number of (or the most critical) objectives.

The objectives of a PPP might include increased coverage, improved services, efficiency improvements with associated reduction in government subsidy, or customer satisfaction. The government and its advisors should use cost-benefit analysis and consult a wide range of possible private partners to gain insight on the appeal, or lack of appeal, of the options under consideration.

Particular PPP forms are used more widely and are more readily applied to particular sectors. For instance, BOT is more often employed in the development of toll roads and wastewater plants while management contracts might be used in healthcare services.

However, no PPP option can be applied without tailoring it to the local context. The options provide a menu of contract types that can be modified to suit specific project requirements. Incorporating different components of different contract types or using several contracts in combination may be necessary. Additional modifications may be necessary to facilitate the financing of the transaction, to respond to concerns of potential partners, to improve low-income service provision, and to address labour issues.

The identification process determines the status of the sector undergoing reform. Each form of PPP has a set of pre-requisites for successful implementation. For instance, deeper forms of PPP that transfer greater risk to the private sector will require more sophisticated legal and regulatory structures, as well as availability of local skills to implement and monitor the transactions. Other constraints may be low-cost recovery levels, lack of system information, or poor technical performance. If prerequisites are not in place as determined through the identification, it may be prudent to start with a less extensive form of PPP. An alternative would be to achieve PPP pre-requisites during the preparatory phase by implementing legal and regulatory reforms, ensuring key investments are made.

A particular option such as a concession may best meet the objectives of the government, but the level of risk may be unacceptable to potential private investors. The likely level of interest can be assessed through analysis of previous investments in the region, country, and sector, and by assessing the market interest.

Prior to the formal procurement process, potential bidders are often invited to comment on a proposed project structure. The comments are based on a pre-bid road show, a briefing, or a project paper, which is shared. Often, the opportunity is described as an *information memorandum*, a summary of the key attributes of the project, the operating environment, and anticipated financing. These discussions also generate market interest in an opportunity and may broaden the pool of potential bidders. Collecting this market feedback from potential private partners during the design/preparatory phases ensures that the bid package attracts interest.

Based on above considerations, the available options can be ranked and the government can take an informed decision on the PPP strategy to be adopted.

5

Preparatory Work for PPP Projects

After selecting the appropriate option for PPP, the preparatory work starts. It addresses the following constraints identified through sector analysis:

1. Legal and regulatory frameworks.
2. Technical preparations.
3. Readiness of institutional set-up.
4. Commercial, financial, and economic preparations.
5. Involvement of stakeholders.
6. Inclusion of local partners.
7. Labour considerations

The preparatory stage culminates in the achievement of an environment conducive to sustainable reform and in a well-defined, documented, and agreed upon PPP process.

5.1 Legal and Regulatory Frameworks

Potential PPP project will exist with a public policy framework, which includes specific legal and regulatory settings.

Legal analysis encompasses the inventory of existing laws, regulations, contracts, and other legal documents that define the characteristics of PPP or those that have to be changed. Gaps are also identified where new legal instruments are required. These may relate directly to PPP (privatization law, sector licensing etc.)—or be of more broad and general relevance (company law, labour laws, environmental laws, foreign exchange regulations etc.).

Thus, the PPP structure has to reflect the prevailing tax regime, concession rights, dispute resolution procedures, public service laws, labour laws etc. Corporate structures have to adhere to company laws and other legal requirements. To the extent that laws have to be changed to accommodate the desired PPP, the timetable should reflect a realistic period for this. The legal work continues as the PPP process progresses.

Similarly, the regulatory regime including oversight arrangements for pricing, customer service, operations, and market structure may need to be changed or newly created. The desired PPP option has to be contrasted with the existing regulatory arrangements and capacity and regulatory gaps should be filled or the PPP structure should be changed. The gaps may include the need for: (i) more explicit regulations and requirements of the operator (to be embedded in contract, regulations, or statute), (ii) developing actual regulatory institutions (such as an independent regulator, a regulatory unit within government, and contracting of regulatory capacity), (iii) training regulators; and (iv) developing procedures whereby the regulator requests and receives information.

The roles of each entity involved in PPP project should be described and justified by assigned authorities.

5.2 Technical Preparations

The technical design of a project starts with identification of desired coverage targets and service standards. From these starting points, estimating the cost of these desired services and cost recovery tariffs is possible. Government has the option of putting these cost recovery tariffs in place, subsidizing cost recovery, or revisiting the initial targets and service standards.

The technical specifications of the proposed PPP project need to be defined and documented in the terms of reference, and ultimately enshrined in the PPP contract. The preparation stage is the time to develop the preliminary specifications. Development of the final technical specifications of a project is an iterative process which builds on feedback from the market and the affordability of the project at each design stage.

The technical preparation builds on the analytical work that has been done in preparing the sector analysis and road map, including demand analysis, asset inventory, and investment analysis.

The technical terms of reference enable bidders to understand required outputs, quantify necessary investment, and estimate resulting operating performance. Technical terms of reference need to strike a balance between being too narrow/restrictive and too loose. Technical specifications that are too narrow may mean that a bidder is prohibited from using the most economical technical solution. Too loose terms may lead to proposals that diverge significantly from each other and are hard to compare and rank. A strategy for dealing with this dilemma is to focus on defining the technical outputs expected rather than dictating the inputs to be employed, thus allowing the bidders some reasonable latitude to determine the most efficient way to achieve outputs.

5.3 Readiness of Institutional Set-up

When sector restructuring is part of the PPP process, the private sector is engaged to undertake activities that were earlier in the public domain. In the changed scenario, the public sector becomes a regulator or monitor, playing a limited role in actual service provision, if any. Most countries initially lack the institutions and institutional capacity required to organize, manage, and implement a PPP process. Existing institutions need to build capacity to be able to take on new roles and new institutions often have to be created. Some key institutional arrangements used to support PPP are: (a) PPP units, (b) project implementation unit, and (c) technical assistance.

5.3.1 PPP Unit: A PPP unit is established as a point of co-ordination, quality control, accountability, and information related to PPP either within a single sector or across a range of sectors. These units are created as a new agency or within a ministry, which is closest to the sector to be reformed. For private proponents, the units provide transparency and consistency. For public stakeholders and the public at large, the units are able to disseminate information and provide specialized management of a specialized process. The units serve to ensure that the key stakeholders relevant to a PPP adhere to a consistent methodology and agreed guidelines. PPP units have typically focused on the identification, development, and bidding of projects. However, focus is increasing on the potential role units may play in the oversight of a contract once launched. This may include ensuring that the proper systems are in place for monitoring and reporting.

The units should command the right level of authority and should be led by a well-respected and competent executive. The units need not be large. In fact, large units can undermine the intent of PPP to promote efficiency. The units often require initial or ongoing technical assistance from PPP specialists. PPP activity may occur on a national or sub-national level and the location of the PPP units should correlate to the market activity. There must also be coordination with the sector ministry associated with a particular PPP, particularly the project implementation unit.

5.3.2 Project Implementation Unit (PIU): A PIU is a vehicle to plan and implement a project or projects. At times, it is linked with a line ministry, but it can also be quasi-independent of the ministry. Most PIUs are established to support large capital investment projects and the life span of the PIU is linked with the project life cycle. The precise structure and role of a PIU will depend on the requirements of the funding agency and the executing agency, the type of project, and the local context.

The advantages to developing a PIU are the creation of a central point of accountability and management. The PIU typically monitors and reports on project progress, performs financial management and accounting, and handles project procurement. Where both PIU and PPP units exist, close and regular coordination is needed.

5.3.3 Technical Assistance: Unless the government is deeply experienced in contracting PPPs, there will be occasions to hire transaction advisors and/or specialist advisors such as lawyers, financial analysts, financiers, economists, sociologists, and sector specialists to support the government. These advisors can be procured as a team or recruited individually, in which case co-ordination among the team members should be ensured. Advisors pay an important role in maintaining momentum, developing strategies for government consideration, helping develop public messages and information, performing analysis of PPP options, and supporting the bidding and negotiation processes. The specialist advisors should be brought into the process early and should be paired with government counterparts. As PPP is considered, government should be identifying potential local counterpart staff, developing a PPP unit or PIU, and should be training staff to take on new responsibilities. The local capacity building should be supported through working relationships with any advisor.

Technical advisors should continue support through contract signing and possibly beyond. The bid and negotiation process involves repeated clarifications and iterations of the bid documents, often occurring swiftly. The process must be well-organized, politically defensible, and must lead to a good outcome. If external support (financial, legal, and technical) to the government is not available at this stage, key government officials must receive training in negotiations and be completely familiar with the content and intent of the bid package.

5.4 Commercial, Financial and Economic Preparations

In designing and preparing PPP, there must be a process to balance service levels with the tariff levels, creating a package of price and service which is acceptable to customers and sustainable for the utility. Critical to this analysis is the structure of payments to and revenues for the private partner, including any subsidies that might be required.

This process will encompass the following:

1. Technical analysis to determine the cost of service.
2. Market and social research to determine what people are willing and able to pay for certain service levels.

3. Financial analysis and modelling to determine the cost recovery tariff required to support the desired coverage targets and service levels.
4. Consultation and trade-offs to agree any transitional subsidies until cost recovery is achieved or ongoing subsidies, e.g., to low-income customers. If the subsidies are not available, coverage and service targets may need to be reduced.

The financial model must be flexible enough to accommodate a range of variables, allowing for an iterative process between the financial modelling and the PPP design. A key objective should be to ensure the financial sustainability of the utility through efficiency gains and through balancing of income and expenses. The financial model is a tool that helps achieve the right balance of affordability, cost recovery, and investment. The model will help prioritize investments and inform decisions on who should pay for investments, depending on the respective cost of capital. Some countries also find it useful to use a public sector comparator (PSC) model which helps government test whether a private investment proposal offers value for money compared with the most efficient form of public provision.

In preparing the transaction, there are 4 important considerations:

1. Sources of project financing.
2. Tariff design.
3. Tariff adjustments.
4. Design and application of subsidies.

5.4.1 Sources of Project Financing: Infrastructure PPPs typically require financing; that is, external funds are required for the initial investment costs that are recovered over time from future revenue streams. The funds may be sourced from the public sector or the private sector. Regardless of the source of finance, such funds have a cost and, therefore, impact the project's economics and required tariffs and thus affordability. Fundamental to the question of project financing is the correlation between perceived credit risk and the cost of finance.

Cost of funding by the government is typically lower than that of a private operator. Providing private financing may therefore increase the financial costs of PPP. However, the efficiency gains from PPP are expected to outweigh this additional cost and result in net savings and efficiency gains, with an ultimate benefit to consumers. In addition, public sector financing is usually scarce.

The operator will typically establish a project company for implementing the contract, often called special purpose vehicle (SPV). The company owners may be a consortium of companies or a single large company. The company owners will not usually finance all project requirements. Instead, they will provide a proportion as equity and borrow the remainder of the required financing from financial institutions or place debt securities in the capital market.

The creditworthiness (*bankability*) of a project depends on a number of factors, some of which are within the control of the government when designing PPP. They include commercially attractive project design and tariffs as well as strong off-take arrangements to reduce market/revenue risk, together with the level of certainty and transparency of regulatory settings, which affect future cash flows.

Project finance is a specialized activity and, depending on prevailing market conditions, may or may not be available at any time. To make financing possible or to secure better borrowing rates, the operator may seek credit enhancement through insurance or guarantees. These might include credit guarantees from the government itself or from a development finance institution and/or political risk guarantees from insurers or development finance institution against the government or regulator not adhering to agreements.

5.4.2 Tariff Design: Tariffs need to balance a number of objectives:

1. Stipulated service standard and associated costs.
2. Customers' willingness and ability to pay.

3. Resulting cost recovery.
4. Return on investment for private operator.
5. Need for/availability of subsidies.

The right combination of factors must be determined through an iterative optimization process using the project model. This process is made more complex if differentiated/complex tariff structures or tariff adjustment mechanisms are used. It is critical to employ qualified and experienced specialists for this modelling and optimization task.

The following objectives provide an appropriate starting point for designing tariffs:

1. Cost recovery/return on investment.
2. Fairness and equity.
3. Simplicity and comprehensibility.

A. Cost Recovery/Return on Investment: The combination of service standards (costs) and tariffs (revenues) determines the commercial viability of a project. Beyond that the private operator has the chance to improve the ultimate financial outcome by being particularly efficient in investment and operations. Therefore, a private operator will get involved in a project only if he expects a fair chance to make a profit given a pre-determined set of service standards and tariffs.

The internal rate of return (IRR) and return on equity (RoE) are the most commonly used measures to assess the financial attractiveness from a private operator's perspective. A private operator will assess the potential IRR of a project against cost of equity, adjusted for the perceived risk of the project. A private operator may be willing to accept a lower IRR if some risks are reduced or mitigated through government actions or otherwise. Revenues are considered adequate if they enable an operator to maintain, replace, modernize, and expand services and assets.

B. Fairness and Equity: As a starting point for determining fairness, tariffs should reflect costs and different customer groups/classes should pay tariffs that reflect the cost of supplying them. Thus, people in similar circumstances pay similar amounts or people accepting lower quality of services should have their bills lowered. However, some services, like water and wastewater services, are often considered a public service, and no customer should be denied access to water on the grounds of poverty. Specific subsidies or cross-subsidies built into the tariff system can address this situation.

C. Simplicity and Comprehensibility: Objective of simplicity and comprehensibility means that tariffs should be easily accessible and understandable to employees and consumers of the utility. If a tariff structure is too complex, customers may not understand the implication of changes in consumption for their bills or the range of options available to them. However, over simplification may result in incentives being lost or a negative impact on fairness.

There is a need to balance these above objectives against one another. There is a further requirement that certain fundamentals be in place including a definition of a reasonable rate of return, an understanding of how assets will be valued, and whether any additional returns are to be allowed. After evaluating these factors and determining the appropriate allocation of risks in PPP, the initial tariff rates and tariff structure are set in place until an adjustment is warranted.

5.4.3 Tariff Adjustments: To expect one set of tariffs to remain viable and appropriate over the typical life of a PPP project is unrealistic. It is, therefore, essential to define practical rules for adjustments. This requires defining the following:

1. The triggers for a price adjustment, such as changes in raw material prices, inflation and exchange rate fluctuations.
2. The mechanisms by which the adjustment will be made, including cost plus and price cap regulations.
3. The frequency of adjustments including cost pass-throughs, tariff indexation, tariff resets, and extraordinary tariff adjustments.

A. Mechanisms: There is a difference between the

regulatory requirements of utilities, such as waste management, electricity, water, and telecommunications, and other forms of public infrastructure, such as roads. Tariff adjustment mechanisms for utilities are discussed below within two basic categories:

1. Cost-plus mechanisms.
2. Price-cap mechanisms.

Cost-plus mechanisms permit regulated firms to pass all operating expenses and capital costs on to the consumer. Under this system, there is no adjustment unless the operator applies to the regulatory authority and requests a review and reset.

The regulator reviews the operator's overall cost base in response to any proposal that higher prices are needed to cover their full costs. In theory, this approach provides the best match of prices to incurred costs, but delivers weaker incentives for efficient operation and development since the recovery of a rate of return is assured.

Cost-plus regulation has the potential to encourage firms to inflate operating costs, rather than pursue efficiency. It nevertheless has a strong element of certainty from an investment perspective, which may mitigate risk.

Price-cap regulation, on the other hand, provides a more direct incentive for efficiency. Price caps are put in place to control the quantum of revenue over a period, but the firms are given leeway to increase earnings through performance improvements. Under this mechanism, a firm can change its price level and its tariff structure according to an index that typically includes an inflation measure. This approach may provide a stronger incentive to improve efficiency and reveals the true costs of providing services.

The choice of regulatory approach is driven by many factors, including the economic expertise available, the accounting and auditing system, investment requirements of a sector, and motivation for efficiency. During the early stages of development when regulatory capacity is being developed, price caps may be a better choice. Prices can be set high enough to attract capital. At a more mature stage of regulation, cost-plus mechanisms might be appropriate to attract large-scale investment.

Many regulatory systems encompass aspects of price-cap and cost-plus mechanisms in a tailored hybrid approach to sector-specific issues.

Nevertheless, the form of regulatory system should be subject to detailed analysis and consideration, which takes account of country, sector, industry, and infrastructure capital investment profiles.

Regulation of non-utility infrastructure PPPs takes a slightly different form and is typically articulated through the PPP contract. Under an infrastructure PPP, the fundamental goal of regulation is to allocate risks rationally and maintain stability between risk and expected return.

B. Frequency of Adjustments: There are different procedures for enacting adjustments in tariffs. In some cases, there is agreement that the costs of certain inputs (e.g. energy) are to be immediately reflected, passed-through, in the tariff charged to and collected from consumers. In this way, the risk of the input price increase is immediately passed on to consumers. Other pass-throughs might include a change in tax rates, or a change in the quality standards imposed by government. The mechanism is appropriate when the service provider has no control over the input. The pass-through may reduce the service provider's incentive to use the input more efficiently, yet the provider is also wary of increasing tariffs beyond what consumers are willing and able to pay.

C. Tariff Indexation: This mechanism is similar to a cost pass-through but uses a different tool to make the adjustment. Rather than the actual costs of the service, the tariffs are adjusted to reflect a change in an index of prices (such as the consumer price index), on a regular timetable. While indexation may protect the provider from price increases that are predictable and within normal limits, the provider is still vulnerable to changes outside the norm or outside the index. In some cases, the indexation formula is based on a basket of prices most relevant to the service being provided.

D. Periodic Tariff Adjustment (Tariff Reset): A more tailored mechanism for adjusting tariffs is the tariff reset. For a long-term PPP, an indexation or pass-through will likely be insufficient to accommodate all sector changes over the life of the contract. Therefore, the rules for tariff resets are defined before PPP is implemented and will be a topic of discussion among all parties relevant to the discussion of allocating risk.

The discussion of tariff resets has to cover: (a) objectives of the reset, (b) methodology for the reset, and (c) triggers for a review and potential reset.

The objectives of the adjustment can include allowing a reasonable rate of return to the operator, encouraging efficiency through a rate of return, or restoring the financial position of the operator who has confronted an unanticipated (and uncontrollable) change in the operating environment such as an exchange rate change.

Depending on the objective of the reset, different methodologies may be used. For instance, there might be an attempt to determine what the most efficient operating costs would bc through benchmarking or obtaining expert advice. If the reset is to restore financial standing to the operator, only key cost variables may require review.

Such a tariff adjustment might be triggered by a request for a review or by a specified event. Typically, these adjustments are allowed on a pre-determined periodic basis, such as every 5 years.

In some cases, highly unusual circumstances such as strife or bankruptcy might trigger an extraordinary price review.

5.4.4 Design and Application of Subsidies: Government subsidies can be used to make a project commercially viable from the perspective of the private operator if the desired combination of service and tariff levels does not result in sufficient cost recovery. This will make sense if the aggregate cost to the government under PPP (including subsidy) is lower than the cost to the government of operating the service fully under the public sector.

Government subsidies can be *general* (i.e. applying to the overall project) or *specific*, in which case they are tied to service provision to deserving consumer segments (e.g. those below poverty line).

Cross-subsidies do not involve government payments but are a compensation mechanism built into the tariff structure. They serve as a means of reducing average tariff charged to one group of customers by increasing the average tariff charged to another group of customers. The most common forms of cross-subsidies include subsidies from non-household to household customers, and subsidies from high-volume customers to low-volume customers, through rising block tariff structures. Subsidies can be established for access (connection charges) or for consumption.

Governments typically provide subsidies to reduce tariff levels for the purposes of helping the poor, addressing public health issues, addressing environmental issues, and/or because of political constraints on raising tariffs.

Different types of subsidies can be used to address different issues. Options are cash subsidies, including output-based aid, cheap capital, and in-kind grants and tax exemptions. Each of these options is described further below.

A. Cash Subsidies: Cash subsidies involve cash payments by the government to the private operator or project company. Payments may be made to cover a portion of investments or can be related to service delivery. Clearly, subsidies should be designed to ensure that the private operator has an incentive to achieve the desired public policy outcome. This is not always easy as subsidies may create perverse incentives for inefficient operations or other undesirable outcomes.

Where there are political constraints to increasing tariffs, a general cash subsidy could be paid to the private service provider to reduce the average tariff required from customers to cover the utility's operating expenses. In this case, setting the size of the subsidy in advance is essential. Not doing so will ensure that the private operator has little incentive to minimize operating expenses. In setting the size of the subsidy in advance, provision might be made for a gradual phasing out of the subsidy, through annual reductions in its size, as operating efficiencies are realized and tariff increases are phased in.

B. Low Cost Capital: This refers to a lowering of the effective cost of borrowing for the private operator. Governments can subsidize the cost of debt to a utility by lending it money at concessional rates (i.e. below its own debt servicing costs). Subsequent write-offs of these loans by government may represent a further subsidy to a utility although this is likely to cause significant problems later when further borrowing may be required. Governments may also subsidize the cost of debt to the utility by providing guarantees or by taking responsibility for exchange rate risk, which can be a significant cost to utilities in developing countries.

C. In-kind Grants and Tax Exemptions: Governments may also provide subsidies to privately operated utilities through in-kind grants and tax exemptions. In-kind grants may take a variety of forms, such as water abstraction rights, which would otherwise be subject to some form of charging regime, or land grants. Tax exemptions are commonly applied to publicly operated utilities and these may be extended once the utility is privately operated.

Again, these subsidies are not targeted to service delivery outcomes or to those customers most in need of assistance. As a result, there will be a leakage of benefits to non-poor households, assuming that these benefits are passed on to customers and are not captured by the operator itself in the form of offsetting cost increases.

In case subsidies are necessary, these forms of subsidy should be evaluated by making comparable estimates of the benefits and costs of each subsidy and assessing how well they achieve their stated objectives, such as targeting the poor.

5.5 Involvement of Stakeholders

The early involvement of all stakeholders in the PPP process helps to develop an enabling environment. The stakeholders provide valuable information on the points of concern, the performance expectations, and potential risks. This input is also critical to assess whether key business assumptions of the proposed PPP are realistic and enforceable. Avoiding consultation invites the risk of later opposition, which slows or derails the process. Ongoing consultation with stakeholders is important at every stage.

Consultation with potential bidders and partners is also critical to ensure that the proposed PPP design meets their requirements. Otherwise, there is a risk that the PPP design includes an unrealistic combination of desirable features that will make the project unattractive to bidders or unsustainable. Collecting informal feedback from the market during the preparation stage is therefore critical. More formal consultations can take place during project implementation.

5.6 Inclusion of Local Partners

From the perspective of the government, including local private and public partners in the PPP process, as much as possible, is generally desirable. There are a variety of ways to achieve this.

5.6.1 Local Private Partners: Local companies are often qualified to be the private partner in PPPs and to develop, improve, and operate infrastructure. Contracts with local partners can range from service contracts to BOTs and may apply to big and small projects. Local partners may be particularly effective for smaller, localized projects, e.g. to reach small towns and peri-urban areas, which demonstrate a viable market, but which are remote from the core infrastructure. Competent utilities or construction firms may enter into competitive tenders to perform discrete services or to construct new facilities.

To encourage and regulate local participation, government

should predetermine a policy on the inclusion of local companies, ensuring against corruption, and setting appropriate and realistic evaluation criteria to enable local companies to compete, while assuring appropriate project quality.

5.6.2 Local Sub-contractors: In sectors such as water and energy where small-scale service providers are prevalent and necessary to fill gaps in the service provided by the dominant utility—at least for the short to medium term—PPP partners may be encouraged to integrate such providers into their strategies. This would not replace intentions to ultimately provide service through formal arrangements, but would prevent the PPP from displacing small-scale providers until such time as replacement services are available.

5.6.3 Local Government Units: Many joint venture arrangements include municipal or other local public partners. This can be an effective way to bring government decision-makers and local stakeholders into corporate governance of the company, transforming their role into one of ownership. There are also possible conflicts of interest in such arrangements, which need to be recognized and mitigated against.

5.7 Labour Considerations

Public sector workers often oppose proposed PPP arrangements. There should be early and constant dialogue among the government, labour unions, and public employees to set out the objectives and strategy for PPP. Information on worker issues should be proactively shared to allay speculation and unfounded concerns. Workers need to be dealt with fairly and either provided with employment opportunities in the new company or given acceptable severance packages. In working through the labour issues associated with PPP, a legal review is critical. This includes public service acts and regulations, laws specific to the sector and the enterprise, collective bargaining agreements, and any precedents in other sectors.

For employees and unions, the key issues will be redundancies or severance payments. This would include the terms under which employees would be laid off and the opportunity to join a new company if one is being created. Public service employees should be advised whether they are to be transferred to any new entity, whether all employees are eligible for severance and possible rehiring, or whether only certain employees will be eligible for severance and/or opportunity with the new company. Employees will need to know the terms of employment with a new company, including salary, reporting lines, benefits, security of tenure, and whether accrued pensions and benefits will be transferred.

Whether an employee is severed or retained, there will be questions about retraining opportunities being offered. As soon as possible, an explicit programme to retrain severed workers, allow for spin off of certain functions, and/or improve the capacity of retained staff should be implemented. The way in which worker issues are handled depends almost entirely on local labour law and local precedent. There should be an attempt to clarify, early in the process, what the law does and does not provide for. Otherwise, speculation will be considerable. Workers should be represented in the process as soon as possible and information should be proactively disseminated.

6

Implementation and Monitoring of PPP Projects

The key activities related to implementing a PPP project and monitoring its progress are discussed below.

6.1 Collecting Feedback from Potential Bidders

Once PPP has been structured and the preparatory work is underway, the transaction manager, responsible for ensuring that the process runs smoothly, transparently, and timely, should be in place. During the transaction stages, it is important to have more formal interaction with potential bidders on the specifics of the transaction as designed. During these interactions, the government needs to guard against potential manipulation of the PPP design and process by the bidder to his advantage.

Likewise, bidders should not enjoy any advantage in the bidding process through such consultations. Discussions must avoid any bias toward a particular bidder and should be broadly held with sector stakeholders as well. The government may find it useful to be supported by PPP advisors in its interactions with potential bidders.

Two specific points of interaction with the potential bidders are as under:

1. Bid conference.
2. Bid document consultation.

6.1.1 Bid Conference: During the bid conference, the government presents an outline of the project and bidders are invited to react and question. However, in a formal setting surrounded by competitors, some bidders may withhold concerns, be unwilling to share good ideas, or may collude with other bidders to push for a particular change.

6.1.2 Bid Document Consultation: Alternatively (or in

addition to a bid conference), bidders may be invited individually to comment on the draft bidding documents, including the draft contract. This approach allows the government to identify issues of concern across the range of bidders. Government should send each bidder a full set of the responses to all questions raised, thus avoiding any semblance of favouritism.

A bidder will expect to have a clear understanding of the time line, the sequence of activities, the decision points, and the decision makers. This information should be given to bidders in writing and should be regularly reviewed and reconfirmed. This clarity is necessary to provide bidders with a sense of confidence in the transparency and reliability of the process.

6.2 Notification and Pre-qualification

The bid package, contracts, and any marketing documents—as well as protocols for communicating with the public and potential bidders—need to be developed. The starting point in the actual procurement process is the public notification of the opportunity and the prequalification of bidders. Different procurement methods entail different activities, but a prequalification process is common to many PPPs. Under this process, an official notification is placed in local and international print and electronic media, advising the public of an opportunity to participate in the project. The content of the advertisement depends on applicable procurement rules. Companies are invited to request a prequalification package and seek access to further information.

An important aspect of information dissemination is the establishment of a data room. Pre-qualified bidders are invited to use this centralized repository of all information related to the PPP project, which is to be available to potential bidders. The information should be organized according to topics and granted equally and fairly to bidders. During a transaction, the room will be staffed by an attendant and bidders must sign and submit to data room rules (e.g. access times, making photocopies, using other technical equipment etc.).

The amount of time and effort required to populate a data room should not be underestimated. Although the accuracy and completeness of the data in the data room are normally not guaranteed, the process organizers and the government nevertheless need to ensure that the data are not false or misleading. Bidders typically apply a degree of scepticism to the veracity of the data. They may question the seriousness of the process if very little data are available.

Prequalification ensures that only bidders with the minimum required expertise and financial strength are able to bid for the opportunity. The prequalification documents usually contain the following:

1. Project information, such as the key characteristics of the project and the operating context.
2. Instructions to bidders outlining the anticipated bid process and evaluation criteria.
3. A list of documents required from the prospective bidders to demonstrate their suitability for the project.

In response, the prospective bidders submit information including the following:

1. Legal status of bidding entity.
2. Experience on comparable projects.
3. Financial status/resources of bidder.
4. Ability to raise financing.
5. Staff and resources to be directed to the project.

A pre-determined scoring matrix should facilitate assessment of the prequalification applications. The matrix sets out each criterion to be scored, the score assigned to each, and the respective weighting. The matrix can include special criteria such as expertise in servicing low-income customers or may prioritize local bidders if desired. It is important to be realistic about the potential pool of bidders and set the threshold sufficiently high to discourage non-serious or unqualified bidders, while maintaining a pool of bidders large enough for effective competition. The prequalification results in a short list of bidders invited to respond to the bidding package.

6.3 Procurement Process

Some initial decisions need to be made regarding the procurement and the bid evaluation process. The choice of procurement method will depend on the government's budget, capacity, desire to encourage innovation, need for high-level inputs, vulnerability to corruption, and objectives of the PPP project. Three main options, distinguished by the level of competition they create, are available:

1. Direct negotiations.
2. Competitive negotiations.
3. Competitive bidding.

6.3.1 Direct Negotiations: Entering into direct negotiations (sole-source process) can save government time and money and may alert government to an unrealized opportunity for PPP. However, sole sourcing can encourage corruption through lack of transparency, and the cost benefits of competitive bidding are lost. Government has to be confident of its negotiation skills and its information to ensure that a sole-source deal is advantageous.

The government needs to ascertain that procurement laws and/or rules permit it to award such a contract based on direct negotiations. There is also an elevated risk that the fairness of the contract award will be challenged at a later stage, e.g. by disappointed potential bidders or by the political opposition. As such, a strategy of direct negotiations could be considered politically risky.

6.3.2 Competitive Negotiations: Competitive negotiations entail inviting a small group of bidders to a structured negotiation. The bidders are aware of the presence of other bidders and there is pressure to obtain the best price. This arrangement is quicker and less expensive than full competitive process and can yield good prices. The selection of bidders to participate can be non-transparent and may not yield the best bidder pool. There is also an elevated risk of corruption. A time-consuming procurement process may be seen as an opportunity cost to the private sector. This needs to be weighed against the degree of and value to transparency.

6.3.3 Competitive Bidding: Most governments have rules requiring some form of competitive bidding for procuring any private sector good or service. In addition, most international lending institutions and assistance organizations require the use of competitive bidding procedures as a condition of any associated loan or technical assistance. Competition is expected to provide transparency in the process and avoid corruption, and ensure a mechanism for selecting the best-value proposal based on criteria set.

The advantages of competition are available only if there is sufficient interest to generate multiple bidders. A failed auction is highly visible and an embarrassment to the government—another reason careful preparation is important.

The competitive bid process can either be one stage or two stages. In the single-stage process, technical and financial bids are submitted simultaneously in response to a request for proposals. In the two-stage process, a technical response is submitted first and comments are provided. In the second stage, a revised technical bid is submitted together with a financial bid. Competitive bidding for basic operation, maintenance, and service contracts can be relatively straightforward as the scope of services is readily defined and often quantifiable. Complex PPPs like BOTs, concessions, and joint ventures are more challenging procurement processes because both the starting information and the result are often unclear.

6.4 Bid Evaluation Process

6.4.1 Initial Decisions: The evaluation process and criteria should be transparent. Transparency is achieved by supplying as much information about the process as possible, and by drawing up procedures that explicitly ensure that all parties are treated equally. Nevertheless, confidentiality during a bid process is also needed so as not to compromise the legitimate commercial interests of the parties.

Bids are typically evaluated in two broad categories: technical and financial. The relative importance of each should reflect the importance in achieving the specified objectives. The project objectives, project design, information in the bid documents, and evaluation criteria should also be consistent.

A first decision point is whether the technical evaluation will be on a pass-fail basis or whether both the technical and financial information will be evaluated and assigned weighted scores. The technical and financial responses are presented in separate envelopes to ensure a discrete evaluation of each component.

6.4.2 Technical and Financial Evaluation: Evaluation criteria should be stated up-front on the bid data sheet. The technical evaluation typically takes into account the following:

1. Quality of the work plan.
- Services to be provided.
- Methodology and approach.
- Meeting performance standards and optimizing incentive compensation.
- Innovations and improvements.
- Training.
2. Quality of staffing plan.
- Detail of staffing plan.
- Appropriate experience reflecting required services in staffing plan.
- Professional qualifications and experience of key staff as shown in curricula vitae.

The financial evaluation is based on the following:

1. Bid prices as readout (currencies, amounts, and modifications or comments).
2. Corrections for: (a) computational errors and (b) provisional sums.
3. Corrected bid price.
4. Exchange of bids to single currency.
5. Formula for scoring bids if weighted technical/financial evaluation.

6.5 Bid Package

Depending on the type of contract and the local requirements, a bid package can range from several volumes of material to a concise document. The elements listed below are the basic components of a generic bid package.

6.5.1 Invitation for Bids: This is a short 1 to 2 pages document that provides an overview of the opportunity, specifies the deadline for bids to be submitted, and provides information for bidders to use in obtaining the full-bid package. An invitation for bids is typically published in relevant national and international newspapers.

6.5.2 Instruction to Bidders: This provides general instructions to bidders regarding the opportunity, the contents of the bidding documents, preparation and submission of bids, bid opening and evaluation, the bidder's conference or pre-bid meeting, and award of contract.

6.5.3 Bid Data Sheet: The bid data sheet expands on the information provided in the instruction to bidders, indicating any special circumstances or conditions that the bidders must keep in mind. The data sheet also provides the bidders with specific details regarding: (a) where to submit bids, (b) request for clarifications, (c) whom to contact regarding negotiations, (d) the number of copies of the bid to be submitted, (e) any special instructions regarding certifications or powers of attorney, (f) the amount of bid security and (g) evaluation criteria.

6.5.4 Draft Form of Contract: The bid package includes a copy of the draft contract to provide the bidders an opportunity to comment on or mark up the contract. Such a process reduces the amount of time required for contract negotiations by ensuring that bidders agree to the form of contract prior to contract award.

6.5.5 Sample Forms and Procedures: The package includes standard forms which may include, but shall not be limited to, bid forms and price schedules, a bid security form, form of contract agreement, performance security forms, and bank guarantee forms.

In addition to contents above, and depending on requirements of any donors involved in a project, the package may include information on restrictions governing eligibility to bid.

6.6 Essential Elements of a Contract

Regardless of the option selected, the essential elements to be included in a contract can be listed as under:

1. Parties to the agreement.
2. Scope, territorial jurisdiction, and duration of the agreement.
3. Objectives of the contract.
4. Circumstances of commencement, completion, modification, and termination of contract.
5. Rights and obligations of the contractor.
6. Rights and obligations of the government.
7. Insurance requirements to provide security for the insurable matters.
8. Government warranties.
9. Private sector warranties.
10. Consequences of a change in law.
11. Service quality, performance, and maintenance targets and schedules.
12. Procedures for resolving disputes.
13. Indemnification circumstances.
14. Conflict of interests and dispute resolution.
15. Interaction mechanisms between the parties to the PPP contract to go forward.

This list is illustrative and does not capture every clause required in a contract. The final contents of the contract will depend on the project scope, local legal requirements and precedent, and advice of legal experts.

6.7 Negotiations and Contract Start

Ideally, the bulk of issues should be sorted out during the bid process. However, negotiations present the last opportunity to work through contractual issues and both sides may have postponed issues to be dealt with at this last stage. The government side is often the less experienced of the parties at the negotiation table and it is important that it is supported by appropriate advisory expertise.

Only critical personnel should attend negotiations and minutes of the issues covered must be kept. Negotiations should be scheduled with sufficient time for preparations. Several rounds may be needed to conduct negotiations.

Negotiations should not reopen items previously dealt with or should not undermine the integrity of the bidding process by deviating from the original proposal.

Part of the negotiations will focus on conditions precedent, i.e. the conditions to be met by both sides to declare the contract operational. The time-table and process for transition should also be discussed. These discussions should cover the following:

1. Registration actions such as the legal incorporation or registration of any joint ventures or project specific companies.
2. Payment of bonds and guarantees.
3. Worker transitions (i.e. terminal benefits, collective bargaining agreements, redundancies etc.).

6.8 Key Implementation Issues

Moving into implementation, several key considerations for the project partners will help ensure success:

6.8.1 Communication during Implementation: The need for effective communication with stakeholders does not end with contract award. Instead, the early stages of a project are a critical time for the winning bidder to establish the trust of the communities facing development. As the PPP moves into implementation, the selected bidder should have a well-detailed plan for ongoing communication with the community, including an appointed liaison.

6.8.2 Right People on Both Sides of the Relationship: The key staff should have the right technical and managerial skills and an established protocol for working together. Both parties should be well familiar with the details of the contract and both should strive for an atmosphere of mutual trust and respect.

6.8.3 Ability to Manage Variations: The management of PPP contracts requires some flexibility on both sides and a means to adapt the terms of the contract to reflect inevitable changes in the operating environment that could not have been anticipated or dealt with in the contract. Contracts should be capable of change (terms, requirements, scope, etc.) and the relationship should be strong and flexible enough to facilitate it. Good contract management is not reactive, but aims to proactively anticipate and respond to the business needs of the future.

6.9 Measuring, Monitoring, and Reporting on PPP Projects

A successful PPP depends on the capacity of the government to keep the contract on track. This entails setting clear requirements of the partnership, monitoring the performance of all parties to the contract, reporting on results, and enforcing contract provisions that are not met.

Different entities can support or take responsibility for monitoring progress against the targets specified in a contract. These entities are described below.

6.9.1 Contract Monitoring Unit: In some cases, a separate regulator does not exist or is not required. In this case, a special unit can be established within government to receive and verify reports on progress against the contract terms. This unit may be located within the sectoral ministry or a more independent ministry such as finance. To accomplish contract monitoring, the contract has to contain explicit details on the targets, acceptable procedures of measuring performance results, and the reporting regime. In addition, the unit may develop a procedures manual for verifying performance and responding to any contract deviations.

Where incentive payments are to be rendered, the unit should also have a method for ascertaining the basis for such payments, making payment, and reporting on and accounting for payments made.

6.9.2 Regulator: Where a regulator is present, the process is approximately the same as above, but the monitoring is related to the provisions of sector regulations. This means overarching principles and methodologies are set out in regulations and the implementation detail is contained in the contract and a license, if applicable.

The regulator has the mandate to monitor compliance, publish reports on performance, and enforce any penalties for non-performance. Like a contract monitoring unit, the regulator must have procedures manual to dictate the application of its responsibilities.

6.9.3 Independent Auditors: Some countries find it advantageous to procure the services of independent technical and/or financial auditors. This may be in addition to or instead of the role of the contract monitoring unit or regulator. In some cases, the auditor provides an independent assessment of the performance, which provides credibility and support to the overall monitoring. In other cases, this contracted expertise replaces the need to retain an ongoing regulatory function.

An important role of any of the above entities is to report on performance. This is accomplished through websites, published reports, reports to parliament, and information made available to customers.

While these entities initially employ international experts to strengthen capacity, the goal in the long-run is to transit to fully local staff. This can be accomplished through training with regional and international peers, often from a regional perspective.

7

Poor-friendly Aspects of PPP

The final objective of all economic efforts is human development which encompasses quality of life, the level of well-being and access to basic social services. Under PPP model, the private sector is seen as a potential source of expertise, efficiency, and capital, which are required to improve and expand services, but which are often lacking in the public sector. In many cases, the private sector has been able to successfully partner with public utilities to the advantage of consumers. However, experience has shown that many private operators were unable or unwilling to improve or expand services to low-income groups (LIGs), or in the Indian context below poverty line (BPL) households. The underlying cause is that the private sector may have little incentive to extend services to low-income areas due to the high cost of providing the service and low profits due to lack of a payment culture, lack of tenure, low consumption, and low-cost structures for those customers.

The concerns voiced by consumers, non-government organizations (NGOs), and representatives of civil society have translated into new, targeted approaches to the needs of LIGs within the rules of PPP structures. The most explicit of these approaches is a new approach called output-based aid (OBA). However, there are other ways in which the PPP process and the basic forms of PPP can be approached from a pro-poor perspective. When this approach is combined with tailored interventions to alleviate service constraints, PPPs can provide adequate incentives to the private sector and balance the financial and social risks.

7.1 Poor-friendly Characteristics of PPP Options

Re-examining the range of options and any inherent

advantages or disadvantages in terms of service to the poor is important. Then it is possible to consider specific pro-poor interventions that might be attached to a process. As a component of a reform package, a PPP can be tailored to address specific reform objectives. The PPP process and contract can therefore be tailored, more or less, to the requirements of BPL households to the degree desired and feasible.

7.1.1 Service and Management Contracts: The operator has no responsibility to finance operations or to invest in the system and payment is not fully tied to the amount of tariff revenue collected. All resources, apart from specific expertise, are provided by the public sector, and the operator can only make best use of those resources provided.

As the operator has no responsibility to invest in the system, these contracts, by their very nature, cannot require the operator to extend or provide service to low-income areas. However, the contracts can require expertise in social issues and in developing and implementing any funded low-income strategies.

7.1.2 Lease and Affermage Contracts: It is possible to structure compensation incentives into a lease that encourages providing service to BPL households within the served area. However, extension of the system into unserved areas remains with the public sector (or as negotiated) and may not be a priority for either public or private sector. If the low-income areas fall within the existing service area, the operator may be motivated to provide service for the sake of increasing tariff revenue or remuneration. However, these areas may be a lesser priority than other consumer groups within the service area.

7.1.3 Concessions: Concessions provide the operators with an inherent incentive to provide service to as many customers as possible. Under the compensation scheme of a concession, the operator is allowed to keep most or all of tariff revenues at an agreed rate (or formula) for a unit of water. The operator thus is motivated to sell as much water as possible, potentially to poor as well as to others.

However, the operator also has an incentive to keep operating costs as low as possible to maximize the profit margin. The operator will thus seek low-cost ways to provide service and may be reluctant to expand the network, particularly into areas that are geographically challenging or where the culture of payment is uncertain.

Related to the compensation issue is the scope of a concession. Under this contract type, the operator typically has the obligation to finance and operate not only the existing system, but also any expansion of the system. Relevant to the poor, the operator would have to determine through cost-benefit analysis that expansion to unserved areas will generate a sufficient return on investment. If the government wants a concessionaire to prioritize expansion to low-income areas, this should be specified in the contract or an incentive should be provided.

7.2 Poor-friendly Interventions

To encourage the operator to serve the poor under PPP, it is vital to consider low-cost mechanisms of providing service, pricing structures that encourage customer payment, low-cost financing for system extension, and other contract mechanisms relevant to the specific characteristics of the low-income population.

PPP arrangements might be made more responsive to the requirements of low-income consumers in many ways. These include both contract provisions or contents and changes in the overall approach to the reform agenda.

7.2.1 Reform Framework: It should focus on the following:

1. The policy commitment to poor must be clarified and strengthened.
2. There needs to be common agreement on which segments of the population constitute poor, as well as which institutional entity is responsible for updating the definition of poor and monitoring their access to service.

3. Current data should be collected on poor in terms of service, preferences, and access. These data should be used to frame strategies and coverage targets and set a baseline for measuring progress. Consultation within the low-income community should be ongoing to understand current service levels, constraints, and preferences.
4. The existence of any legal prohibitions against serving informal settlements or to tailoring service standards to the constraints of a community should be re-examined.

7.2.2 Financial Considerations: These are as under:

1. Government's policy on subsidies should be re-examined in the context of cost recovery goals under PPP.
2. There should be consideration of whether connection fees are a greater disincentive to network service than the ongoing payments for service. If so, the connection fee should be re-examined in terms of level and application.
3. Mechanisms to facilitate payment—such as pre-paid meters, increased pay-points, frequent billing, and others—should be considered.

7.2.3 PPP Contract: It should include the following:

1. The contract should include the flexibility to implement the right level of service appropriate to the financial capability of the poor, with potential to upgrade.
2. Technology and construction standards should be appropriate but low cost.
3. Potential for the poor to contribute in-kind through labour should be considered.
4. Contract should allow for partnership or co-existence with small-scale providers or communities where appropriate to reach a particular low-income group.

7.2.4 PPP Bid Process: It involves the following:

1. If bidders have an obligation in terms of pro-poor service, they require reliable data to that effect.
2. Bidders can be required to present their past experience in serving low-income groups and to explain their present strategy under the PPP contract at hand.

7.3 Output-Based Aid (OBA) Contracts

OBA provides a way in which international financial institutions can directly structure its financing to benefit poor people, even when the service provider is a private company. OBA is the use of explicit, performance-based subsidies funded by the donor to complement or replace user fees. It involves the contracting out of basic service provision to a third party—such as private companies, NGOs, and even public service providers—with subsidy payment tied to the delivery of previously specified outputs. This means that targeted and valuable subsidies to disadvantaged populations are funded through donor funds. The private partner, meanwhile, can only recover this funding by achieving specific performance outcomes. A global multi-trust fund called Global Partnership for Output Based Aid was created in 2003 to provide increased access to reliable basic infrastructure and social services to the poor in developing countries.

Generally, OBA schemes finance the following three types of subsidies:

1. **One Time:** These would include subsidies for connections with the collected user fees covering longer-term operation and maintenance costs. These have been the most common under OBA schemes to date.
2. **Transitional:** Transitional subsidies are used to ease the transition to full cost recovery tariffs.
3. **Ongoing:** Ongoing subsidies are linked to a sustainable source of funding such as general tax revenues, earmarked tax revenues, or explicit cross-subsidies. These subsidies are used to complement the existing funding source. This has been less used and requires longer disbursement periods.

OBA also transfers risk to the operator in several ways. First, OBA links payment of the subsidy to performance outcomes, maintaining pressure on the operator to reach agreed upon service and commercial targets. Second, OBA schemes determine and pay the total level of subsidy ex-post. Thus, the operator runs some risk that payment will not be made by government as agreed.

Typically, OBA payments relevant to pro-poor service would be linked to outcomes related to consumption and coverage expansion, but OBA schemes are also applied to BOT projects that might have an indirect, positive impact on the poor.

To pay out an accurate subsidy under OBA, there has to be a process for monitoring and verifying delivery of the specified outputs.

Part II
Public-Private-Partnership (PPP) Model in India

8

Institutional and Financial Support for PPP in India

Public-private-partnership in India is defined as a commercial legal partnership between government and a private organisation. The Government of India is promoting public-private-partnership (PPP) as an effective tool for bringing private sector efficiencies in creation of economic and social infrastructure assets and for delivery of quality public services. Traditionally, infrastructure development used to occur through the public sector. However, given the scarcity of public resources, and the need to shift scarce public resources into health and education, efforts have been made to induct private participation in the development of infrastructure. These efforts have met with a fair degree of success.

India has systematically rolled out a PPP programme for the delivery of high-priority public utilities and infrastructure and developed what is perhaps one of the largest PPP programmes in the world. As per the 2015 Infrascope Report of the Economist Intelligence Unit, "Evaluating the Environment for PPPs in Asia-Pacific 2014", India ranks first in the world in "Operational Maturity" for PPP projects, third for sub-national PPP activity and fifth overall in terms of having an ideal environment for PPP projects.

The Government of India recognizes several types of PPPs, including user-fee based BOT model, performance-based management/maintenance contracts and modified design-build (turnkey) contracts. Today, there are hundreds of PPP projects in various stages of implementation throughout the country. In the face of ambitious and enormous investment in the infrastructure sector in the coming years, the Government of India is actively promoting PPPs in many sectors of the economy.

There has been a huge gap in the demand and supply of essential social and economic infrastructures and services. These infrastructure shortages are key constraint in sustaining and expanding India's economic growth and making it more inclusive for the poor. Given the large resource requirements for investment and the budgetary constraints, Government of India has been encouraging private sector investment and participation in all sectors.

Over the years, a PPP eco-system has developed, and currently it comprises institutions, developers, financiers, equity providers, policies and procedures.

8.1 Economic and Social Infrastructure Deficit in India

India's infrastructure deficit—whether congested roads and ports, inadequate hospitals or wastewater treatment facilities, and slow trains—is a key factor in constraining economic growth and jobs creation, thereby imposing huge costs on society. Low productivity, poor competitiveness, and high costs are some of the consequences of this deficit.

There is absolutely no time to lose in addressing this deficit with every possible means available to the Government. India will be the world's most populated country before 2030, outgrowing China. Without sustained rapid economic growth and the resulting productive jobs, India will be unable to convert its demographic transition into a demographic dividend. This demographic dividend—a very large working population supporting a relatively small non-working population—has propelled other countries to prosperity and higher incomes. Whether GDP and employment grow rapidly or not, India will have the world's largest working-age population and thereafter the world's largest elderly population. For India to earn its demographic dividend, young Indians must have productive jobs, earn well, accumulate wealth, and save for their old age.

India already represents the largest PPP market in the world as the government has sought to leverage the three roles of PPP infrastructure: (a) generate real efficiency gains through construction management and operational efficiency; (b) bring innovation and creativity by infusing new technology and superior management practices; and (c) help accelerate the closing of the infrastructure deficit by attracting private funding much faster than the years it would take to deploy government funds without breaching fiscal targets.

There is also a pressing need to harness the potentially large supply of global funding for infrastructure. In the developed world, populations are aging, with more savings than ever before in the form of pension, insurance and other institutional funds that are looking for stable, long-term returns that infrastructure investments in India could ideally offer. If India can improve the performance of its PPP markets and attract long-term debt and fixed income products, it can easily take advantage of this sweet spot where savings in the developed world can meet a part of its large need for infrastructure investment.

An adequate supply of high-quality infrastructure and its efficient management and operation over the next few decades can drive rapid economic growth that can generate productive jobs needed to employ the world's largest young labour force. Productively employed, Indian workers can earn, save, and accumulate wealth. There is then every chance that India can indeed become rich before it gets old.

Infrastructure can support economic growth in two ways. First, the direct effect is the sectoral contribution of infrastructure to GDP through backward and forward linkages. Transportation services, for example, are produced in their own industries, with backward and forward linkages and corresponding contributions to output and growth. Greater road capacity tends to lower the cost of transport services for manufacturing, improves the sector's profitability, and thus provides an incentive to raise manufacturing output.

Second, infrastructure investments also produce indirect but significant spill over effects or externalities. Lower transport costs may create economies of scale and scope that lead, for example, to better inventory or supply chain management. Economists measure this indirect efficiency effect of infrastructure as total factor productivity growth—the unexplained residual left over once the contributions of machinery, human capital, and the working-age population have been accounted for in GDP growth.

Infrastructure is not only a direct supplier of jobs, but also has positive externalities for other sectors of the economy, which in turn increases demand for labour in these sectors.

8.2 Importance of PPP for Infrastructure Development

PPPs in infrastructure represent a valuable instrument to speed up infrastructure development in India. This speeding up is urgently required for India to grow rapidly and generate a demographic dividend for itself and also to tap into the large pool of pension and institutional funds from aging populations in the developed countries.

Investment in infrastructure in India has posed a challenge in the last few years. Not only are there reports of delayed or stalled infrastructure projects but the rate of growth of gross fixed capital formation (GFCF) has also been disappointing. Inadequate acceleration in private sector projects has been attributed, inter alia, to unfavourable market conditions, lack of appetite for fresh investment by promoters and delays in obtaining environmental clearances. In the public sector, on the other hand, the slowdown in delivery of projects has been attributed to regulatory decisions, problems in land acquisition and scarcity of funds.

The Union Finance Minister, in his Budget Speech of 2015-16, emphasized the need for increasing public investment in infrastructure. Simultaneously, while referring to the importance of drawing in the private sector, he emphasized the need for a review of the PPP model of infrastructure development, which harnesses private investment for providing public assets and services.

PPP has been accepted as an important policy instrument

for Central and State Governments in the implementation of commercially viable projects.

The high economic growth witnessed by India in recent years has been accompanied by realization of the need for enhanced investment in infrastructure. Rapid urbanization and industrial growth has led to demand for basic infrastructure such as water supply and sanitation, transportation and energy. Rapid growth in purchasing power in the rural areas has simultaneously meant a need for improving connectivity and services for attaining a seamlessly integrated network of logistics and facilities. In order to augment economic growth, the Government has initiated several policy and enabling measures to support the creation of high-quality infrastructure and efficient delivery of services to its citizens.

The use of PPP an as instrument of procurement for creation of infrastructure assets and delivery of public services has been recognized globally. Given the enormity of investment required and the limited availability of public resources for investment in physical infrastructure in India, the projected infrastructure requirements have made it imperative for the Government to explore avenues for increasing investment in infrastructure through a combination of public investment and the PPP mode of delivery.

While augmenting delivery and financing of public projects, PPPs are expected to bring in new and cost-effective technology for creation of infrastructure assets, managerial efficiency, and superior competencies in service standards for the operation and maintenance of public assets. There is a contractual accountability for the private party to guarantee timely and high-quality infrastructure services to end users.

Presently, India offers the world's largest market for PPPs. It has accumulated a wealth of experience in getting to this premier position. As the PPP market in infrastructure matures in India, new challenges and opportunities have emerged and will continue to emerge. Periodic reviews of PPPs are a must to help address issues before they become endemic and to mainstream innovations and foster new ones that improve the successful delivery of PPP projects. This has to be a dynamic process. Such reviews should ideally therefore be done frequently.

India's success in deploying PPPs as an important instrument for creating infrastructure in India will depend on a change in attitude and in the mind-set of all authorities dealing with PPPs, including public agencies partnering with the private sector, government departments supervising PPPs, and auditing and legislative institutions providing oversight of PPPs. This change in attitude requires the following:

1. Moving away from a narrow focus on transactions to focussing on the relationship and on service delivery for citizens.
2. Building an approach of *give and take* between private and public sector partners.
3. Developing a mechanism for dealing with uncertainties inherent in long-time contracts.

Implementation of projects under PPP frameworks should be based on an equitable partnership between different stakeholders in a manner that best delivers services to the citizens of India.

8.3 Origin and Evolution of PPP Model in India

Infrastructure in India is poor when compared to similarly developed nations. The Government of India has identified public-private-partnership (PPP) as a way of developing the country's infrastructure. During India's first liberalization wave in the 1990s, there were various attempts to promote PPPs. However, in some sectors—such as water and sanitation—it failed. India was perceived as too risky and there was significant opposition to private sector involvement. It is only in the first half of the 2000s that the first PPPs were signed and implemented. Construction of infrastructure in India requires large capital outlays and there is a deficit in supply.

In August 2012, Prime Minister Manmohan Singh lifted

the ban on the transfer of government-owned land, relaxed land transfer policy and did away with the need for Cabinet approval for PPP projects in order to accelerate the building of infrastructure.

Evolution of private sector participation in infrastructure can broadly be classified into three phases:

8.3.1 Phase I: It marked the inception of PPPs and saw key projects primarily in the transport and power sectors. However, the early initiatives failed to scale up PPP projects in the absence of an integrated approach, clear policy framework, lack of an institutional mechanism and detailed road map for future growth.

8.3.2 Phase II: This phase, from 2004 to 2011, saw private partnerships scale up significantly. Strong political will to scale up PPP in infrastructure led to the formation of the Committee on Infrastructure chaired by the Prime Minister. This ensured engagement at the highest level of government. Streamlining the appraisal and approval processes as well as standardizing of documents enabled fast roll out of projects. Launch of new initiatives like the Viability Gap Funding (VGF) Scheme, setting up of India Infrastructure Finance Company Limited (IIFCL) helped increase financial flexibility and capacity in the ecosystem. Performance during the Eleventh Five Year Plan (2007-2012) exceeded expectations when the private sector contributed 36.6 percent of the total infrastructure investment while the total infrastructure investment as a percentage of GDP increased from 5 percent to 7 percent.

8.3.3 Phase III: The current phase has seen a decline in the momentum gained during the second phase. Various issues have led to stalled projects in different stages of award, construction and operation. Significant dilution in important terms of the standard bidding documents, over engineering of project design, aggressive bidding by project developers, financing issues, especially bank funding as well as lack of equity funding led to a series of stalled projects, lack of investor interest and overall slowdown in roll out of PPP projects.

India has witnessed various rollouts of major projects being awarded on the basis of PPP and the Indian PPP programme has emerged as one of the largest globally. In view of the demands placed on the limited fiscal space and the substantial scale of investments required in meeting the infrastructure gaps there remains a need to reinforce the drive to promote private participation through the PPP mode. Towards this end, critical analysis of the factors that undermined the implementation of PPP projects over the last few years and making necessary course corrections is required. The current scenario is conducive to this approach as one can tap the liquid international financial markets, which are flush with cash in the low interest rate environment. It is important to place proper monitoring mechanisms and reinforce various institutional reforms to ensure strict adherence to the set processes to reboot PPPs in the country.

It should be noted that during the period of transition from 100 percent state investment in infrastructure towards increasing participation of the private sector, there will be continued need for state support in many infrastructure projects. Infrastructure investment is particularly risky during the construction period and in the initial years of a project before a clear income stream emerges. The government should, therefore, consciously use its available scarce resources in infrastructure projects which otherwise would not receive adequate funding. This way significant leverage would be obtained in the use of government funds for infrastructure investment. Once a project becomes commercially viable, and income streams become secure, the government should disinvest and reinvest in new projects in the nature of a venture capitalist.

The approach to PPP must remain firmly grounded in principles which ensure that PPP are formulated and executed in public interest with a view to achieving additional capacity and delivery of quality public services at reasonable costs. These partnerships must ensure investment for supplementing scarce public resources while improving efficiencies.

8.4 PPP Cell in the Department of Economic Affairs (DEA)

The Government provides guidance for PPP projects, from the project conceptualization stage to final award in pilots, and supports them post-award through various schemes. Initiatives have been taken to build the capacity of public functionaries and institutions in preparing a pipeline of credible, bankable projects. To deepen the capacity of public functionaries at state and municipal levels, various training initiatives and knowledge transfer modules (such as PPP toolkits) have been developed.

The Department of Economic Affairs (DEA) in the Ministry of Finance, Government of India has been overseeing the development of public infrastructure through the PPP model across the country. Through the DEA, the Government has established institutional mechanisms for streamlining and speedy appraisal of PPP infrastructure projects.

PPP Cell, set up in 2006 in the DEA, is responsible for matters concerning public-private-partnerships, including policy, schemes, programmes and capacity building and all other matters relating to mainstreaming PPPs. It acts as the secretariat for Public-Private-Partnership Appraisal Committee (PPPAC), Empowered Committee (EC), and Empowered Institution (EI) for the projects proposed for financial support through Viability Gap Fund (VGF). The PPP Cell is responsible for policy level matters concerning PPPs, including policies, schemes, programmes, model concession agreements and capacity building. The PPP Cell is also responsible for matters and proposals relating to clearance by PPPAC, Scheme for Financial Support to PPPs in Infrastructure (VGF Scheme) and India Infrastructure Project Development Fund (IIPDF).

8.4.1 Functions of PPP Cell: These are as under:

1. Matters relating to appraisal and approval of Central sector PPP projects, as per the Cabinet approved "Compendium of Guidelines for Central Sector PPPs" and the Delegation of Powers assigned from time-to-time except those in road sector.
2. Matters and proposals relating to clearance by Public-Private-Partnership Appraisal Committee (PPPAC) except those in road sector.
3. Matters and proposals relating to the scheme for financial support to public-private-partnerships in Infrastructure Viability Gap Funding (VGF) Scheme except those in road sector.
4. Matters and proposals relating to the scheme for India Infrastructure Project Development Fund (IIPDF).
5. Developing multi-pronged and innovative interventions and support mechanisms for facilitating PPPs in the country, including technical assistance and programmes from bilateral/multilateral agencies on mainstreaming PPPs and support to State and local governments.
6. Managing training programmes, strategies, exposures for capacity building for PPPs and other matters relating to institution building for mainstreaming PPPs.
7. All international interfaces on PPPs and other matters concerning PPPs.
8. Matters relating to management of PPP related information

In 2011, the DEA published guidelines for the formulation and approval of PPP projects. This was part of an endeavour to streamline PPP procedures and strengthen the regulatory framework at the national level to expedite PPP projects approval, reassure private parties and encourage them to enter into PPPs in India.

PPP Cell has developed a website (located at www.pppinindia.gov.in) to provide key information related to PPP initiatives in India and to share PPP best practices for PPP practitioners whether in Government or the private sector. The website is a repository of policy documents, government guidelines, model documents, project information, information on the institutional mechanisms for appraisal of PPP infrastructure projects, schemes developed for financial support to PPP projects and guidance material and reference documents developed by the PPP Cell.

There is another website (www.infrastructureindia.gov.in), developed by the PPP Cell, which provides information on infrastructure projects implemented in India. The website provides detailed guidelines for appraisal/approval procedures to be followed for central (national) sector PPP projects.

PPP Cell is also responsible for proposals relating to clearance by PPPAC, schemes for financial support to PPPs in infrastructure (VGF schemes) and the India Infrastructure Project Development Fund (IIPDF).

The PPP framework assists in providing systematic and speedy appraisals and approvals of projects. The cell has over time progressively opened more and more sectors for private involvement. It has also promoted levies for user charges and also standardised bidding documents such as the model request for qualifications and the model request for proposals.

8.4.2 Public-Private-Partnership Appraisal Committee (PPPAC): In 2006, the Government of India introduced the appraisal mechanism by setting up PPPAC which responsible for the appraisal of PPP projects in the central sector. The appraisal mechanism for the PPP projects was initiated to "ensure speedy appraisal of projects, eliminate delays, adopt international best practices and have uniformity in appraisal mechanisms and guidelines". The PPPAC comprises the following:

1. Secretary, Department of Economic Affairs (in the Chair);
2. Secretary, Planning Commission (now CEO Niti Aayog);
3. Secretary, Department of Expenditure;
4. Secretary, Department of Legal Affairs; and
5. Secretary of the Department sponsoring a project.

PPPAC is responsible for PPP project appraisal at the central level.

8.4.3 Viability Gap Funding (VGF) Scheme: It was

notified in 2006 to enhance the financial viability of competitively bid infrastructure projects, which are justified by economic returns, but do not pass the standard thresholds of financial returns. Under the scheme, grant assistance of up to 20 percent of capital costs is provided by the Central Government to PPP projects undertaken by any Central Ministry, State Government, statutory entity or local body, thus leveraging budgetary resources to access a larger pool of private capital. An additional grant of up to 20 percent of project costs can be provided by the sponsoring Ministry, State Government or project authority.

8.4.4 India Infrastructure Project Development Fund (IIPDF): While good quality advisory services are fundamental to developing well-structured, viable PPPs, the costs of procuring PPPs and particularly the costs of transaction advisors are significant. Development of robust projects with a sound financial structure and optimal risk allocation is critical for evincing market response in respect of the projects.

IIPDF was created in 2007 in the Department of Economic Affairs, Ministry of Finance, Government of India with an initial corpus of ₹ 100 crore for supporting the development of credible and bankable PPP projects that can be offered to the private sector. The IIPDF provides financial support for quality project development activities. The sponsoring authority will thus be able to source funding to cover a portion of the PPP transaction costs, thereby reducing the impact of costs related to procurement on their budgets. IIPDF helps to finance the cost incurred towards development of PPP projects (which can be significant, and particularly the costs of transaction advisors), up to 75 percent of the project development expenses.

8.4.5 Capacity-building Initiatives: The following measures have been taken by the PPP Cell for capacity building and to promote knowledge transfer to improve the PPP initiatives in India.

1. The national PPP capacity-building programme aims to train government officials in various Central and State Government departments, parastatal agencies and urban bodies.
2. Information dissemination, through the website www.pppindia.com, to provide comprehensive information on the status and extent of PPP initiatives in India. This contains:

- Government guidelines and knowledge products for use by PPP practitioners in various sectors.
- Online PPP toolkits to help with improving decision-making for infrastructure and to structure better PPP projects.

3. Mainstreaming PPPs where support to State and Central PPP Cells is provided through programmes using technical assistants and experts.
4. Knowledge-exchange practices through exposure visits and knowledge-exchange programmes with other countries.
5. Pilots aim to ensure that PPP projects are well-structured, particularly challenging sectors, to develop demonstrable PPP projects, ensure successful bid processes and establish their replication potential.
6. Knowledge products are developed to ensure a high standard of PPP implementation, such as: post-award management guidelines and manuals, reports frameworks for PPP contract renegotiation and a green book for the health sector.

8.4.6 PPP Toolkit: PPP Cell has produced a series of guidance papers and a PPP Toolkit to support project preparation and decision-making processes. The objective is to help improve decision-making for infrastructure PPPs in India and to improve the quality of the PPPs that are developed. The tookit has been designed with a focus on helping decision-making at the Central, State and Municipal levels.

The toolkits cover five infrastructure sectors, namely

highways, water and sanitation (W&S), ports, municipal solid waste management (SWM), urban transport [bus rapid transport systems (BRTS)].

In addition, there is a web-based PPP post-award contract management toolkit to help improve the contract management and project execution of the infrastructure sector related PPP projects in India.

8.4.7 Model Documents and Knowledge Repository: The efforts of the DEA and the erstwhile Planning Commission to mainstream PPPs through a multi-pronged approach to standardization of documents (adaptable to individual projects), have enabled easy adoption of PPP projects and capacity building. The Government of India maintains a repository of concession agreements of executed PPP projects in the country across sectors.

Authorities such as National Highways Authority of India (NHAI) and Department of Shipping have published model documents on their respective website for easy accessibility and reference.

8.5 NITI Aayog

India has undergone a paradigm shift—politically, economically, socially, technologically and demographically—since Independence in 1947. The role of Government in national development has seen a parallel evolution. Keeping with these changing times, the Government of India decided to set up National Institution for Transforming India (NITI Aayog), in place of the erstwhile Planning Commission, as a means to better serve the needs and aspirations of the people of India.

Formed on January 1, 2015 through a Union Cabinet resolution, NITI Aayog is a policy think-tank of the Government of India. It replaced the Planning Commission which was scrapped by the Cabinet on August 13, 2014. NITI Aayog aims to involve the states in economic policy-making for India. It will be providing strategic and technical advice to the Central and the State Governments. The Prime Minister heads the Aayog as its chairperson.

NITI Aayog is designed as a catalyst to the developmental process, nurturing an overall enabling environment, through a holistic approach to development going beyond the limited sphere of the public sector and Government of India. This will be built on the foundations of an empowered role of states as equal partners in national development, operationalizing the principle of co-operative federalism.

NITI Aayog is visualised as a knowledge hub of internal as well as external resources; serving as a repository of good governance best practices, and a think-tank offering domain knowledge as well as strategic expertise to all levels of government. It is a collaborative platform for facilitating implementation—by monitoring progress, plugging gaps and bringing together the various Ministries at the Centre and in States—in the joint pursuit of developmental goals.

Infrastructure and PPP division has been created within NITI Aayog to oversee the development of PPP market in the country and provide policy guidance to the Government. NITI Aayog has prepared a brief on how to strengthen PPP policy framework in the country and has provided its recommendations to the Kelkar Committee for their consideration.

NITI Aayog has recently taken an initiative to offer advice and guidance to the States for implementation of infrastructure projects. A Project Management Unit (PMU) under the Development Support Services for States/UTs (DSSS) programme of NITI Aayog has been set up to handhold States in identification, prioritization, selection, and implementation of PPP projects. Finally, a list of 10 big infrastructure projects that can be developed under PPP mode has been prepared for implementation.

8.6 Summary of Initiatives by the Government of India to Promote PPPs

In order to bridge the infrastructure gap, and to create an enabling environment for private sector investment in infrastructure through PPPs, the Government of India has made a concerted effort to develop a dedicated PPP programme. Several initiatives, through the DEA, have helped to create an enabling system for mainstreaming PPPs. This has been helpful to stakeholders in the PPP space, including private developers, financial institutions and governments at national, state and local levels.

8.6.1 Institutional and Financial Support Mechanism:

1. A dedicated PPP cell was set up in the DEA to serve as the secretariat for the various committees that appraise and approve central sector projects and for innovative interventions and financial support mechanisms for facilitating PPPs in the country, and managing training programmes for capacity building for PPPs.
2. The appraisal mechanism for PPP projects has been streamlined to ensure speedy appraisal of projects, eliminate delays, adopt international best practices and ensure uniformity in the appraisal and guidelines. The notified appraisal mechanism includes setting up of the Public-Private-Partnership Appraisal Committee (PPPAC) responsible for the appraisal of PPP projects in the central sector. These include projects in roads, ports, civil aviation, tourism infrastructure, and housing.
3. Standardized bidding and contractual documents have been notified. These include:

- Model Request for Qualification (MRFQ).
- Request for Proposal (RFP) and RFP for technical consultants.
- MCAs for different sectors including highways (both national and state highways), ports, urban transport (metro), and power sectors.

4. Standardized contractual documents have been prepared and notified, such as sector-specific MCAs, which lay down the standard terms relating to allocation of risks, contingent liabilities and guarantees as well as service quality and performance standards, and standardized

bidding documents such as Model RFQ and Model RFP.

5. The Government has created Viability Gap Funding (VGF) Scheme for PPP projects to help promote the sustainability of the infrastructure projects. This scheme provides financial support (grants) to infrastructure projects, normally in the form of a capital grant at the stage of project construction (up to 20 percent of the total project).
6. India Infrastructure Finance Company (IIFCL) has been set up with the specific mandate to play a catalytic role in the infrastructure sector by providing long-term debt for financing infrastructure projects.
7. India Infrastructure Project Development Fund (IIPDF) was launched in December 2007 to finance the cost incurred towards development of PPP projects. The IIPDF supports up to 75 percent of the project development expenses.

8.6.2 Capacity Building and Mainstreaming of PPPs:

1. A dedicated website for PPPs (www.pppinindia.com), giving comprehensive information on the PPP initiatives and various knowledge resources and government guidelines, has been developed along with a web-enabled database (www.infrastructureindia.gov.in) to provide information on infrastructure projects including PPPs. The database is a repository of information on infrastructure projects and their status of implementation across sectors and regions.
2. As part of wide ranging efforts for knowledge dissemination on PPPs, the DEA has developed online toolkits to help project authorities design and develop projects and has published several knowledge products for PPP practitioners.

8.6.3 Renegotiation of PPP Contracts: A report on the framework for renegotiation of PPP contracts has been developed, with a particular focus on the national highway and major port *concessions*. The report identifies issues and changes needed in the contractual and institutional arrangement post-award of the projects.

8.6.4 Contract Management: Guidance material has been developed for the highways, ports and the education sectors for improving the post-award management of PPPs, with particular focus on day-to-day monitoring and proactive management of key risks to preserve the interests of the users of infrastructure services and the concessioning authority. The manuals have been developed on a step-by-step approach on various activities required to be undertaken at different stages of the project lifecycle. The web-based online toolkits are available in the public domain for easy access on www.pppinindia.com

8.6.5 PPP Pilot Project Programme: DEA also has a PPP Pilot Projects Programme where the process of structuring PPP projects in challenging sectors is hand held by the Central Government to develop demonstrable PPP projects. The objective of the initiative is to develop robust PPP projects and successfully enable bids for them to establish their replication potential in the sectors concerned.

8.6.6 Monitoring of PPP Projects: The Government has recently issued guidelines for monitoring of PPP Projects. These guidelines seek to establish a two-tier institutional mechanism for monitoring of PPP projects that would ensure compliance of the contractual framework contained in the concession agreements with a view to safeguarding the interests of the public exchequer and the users.

PPP system in the country is continuously evolving to meet the many challenges encountered in implementation. PPP projects which are maturing require fulsome response by the government to deal with changes in the contracting landscape, new skills required by all parties, increasing need to respond to often unfounded allegations of collusion, and the need for building changes in financing patterns during the concession period.

To sum up, private investment in infrastructure is being encouraged in an environment which ensures competition and transparency. Protection of public interest is being ensured by institutionalising the necessary frameworks and processes for due diligence, checks and balances. However, it is recognized that unless governance issues—such as those related to competition in service provision, collection of user charges, institutional capacity, regulation, and dispute resolution—continue to be adequately addressed, mobilisation of sufficient resources for the requisite infrastructure investment may not be possible.

Simultaneously, the private sector has also continued to engage with Government as contractors for contracts funded by public expenditure. Some State Governments have formulated laws and policies and set up the necessary institutional structures for streamlining PPPs, thereby formalizing the PPP landscape at a sub-national level.

The measures taken by the Government of India in recent years have resulted in a robust pipeline of projects at different stages of implementation. The sectoral spread of PPPs has been fairly diverse in hard infrastructure sectors such as transport (roads, airports and ports), which has seen the largest share in terms of numbers and success. The new airports at Delhi, Mumbai, Bengaluru and Hyderabad and the large dimension of highway projects are part of the programmatic success of PPPs in the country.

9

Electricity, Coal, and Petroleum

India faces formidable challenges in meeting its energy needs and providing adequate and varied energy of desired quality to users in a sustainable manner and at reasonable costs. The country needs economic growth for human development, which in turn requires access to clean, convenient and reliable energy for all.

India is both a major energy producer and a consumer. It currently ranks as the world's seventh largest energy producer, accounting for about 2.49 percent of the world's total annual energy production. It is also the world's fifth largest energy consumer, accounting for about 3.45 percent of the world's total annual energy consumption. However, owing to its massive population—estimated presently at 1.3 billion which accounts for 16.4 percent of world population—India's per capita energy consumption is one of the lowest in the world.

9.1 Legal/Institutional Framework for Energy Management

Energy is a basic requirement for economic development. Every sector of the Indian economy—agriculture, industry, transport, household—needs inputs of energy. The economic development plans implemented since Independence have necessarily required increasing amounts of energy. As a result, consumption of energy in all forms has been steadily rising all over the country.

Presently, energy needs of the country are looked after by the following 4 Ministries of the Government of India:

1. Ministry of Power.
2. Ministry of Coal.
3. Ministry of Petroleum and Natural Gas.
4. Ministry of New and Renewable Energy.

In addition, there is the Department of Atomic Energy, directly under the charge of the Prime Minister.

Critics have pointed out that each of these agencies is concerned with its own areas of operation, policies and programmes which are not always consistent with each other. Hence, opportunities for inter-linkages and synergy are missing and sub-optimal solutions are the result.

9.1.1 Ministry of Power (MoP): Electricity is a concurrent subject at Entry 38 in List III (Concurrent List) of the Seventh Schedule of the Constitution of India. Thus, Parliament and the State Legislatures have overlapping powers to make laws regarding electricity. Hence, reforms in this sector have to be undertaken by the Central as well as State Governments.

India faces challenges in electrical supply and delivery, and is often unable to meet demand, even in very large cities. MoP is charged with overseeing electricity production and infrastructure development, including generation, transmission, and delivery, as well as maintenance projects. MoP acts as a liaison between the Central Government and state electricity operations, as well as with the private sector. It also oversees rural electrification projects.

MoP became a Ministry on July 2, 1992. Prior to that, it was a Department (the Department of Power) in the Ministry of Power, Coal and Non-Conventional Energy Sources. That Ministry was split into the Ministry of Power, Ministry of Coal, and Ministry of Non-Conventional Energy Sources (renamed the Ministry of New and Renewable Energy in 2006).

MoP is primarily responsible for the development of electrical energy in the country. It is concerned with perspective planning, policy formulation, processing of projects for investment decision, monitoring of the implementation of power projects, training and manpower development and the administration and enactment of legislation in regard to thermal, hydro power generation, transmission and distribution. MoP is also responsible for the

Administration of the Electricity Act, 2003, the Energy Conservation Act, 2001 and to undertake such amendments to these Acts, as may be necessary from time to time, in conformity with the policy objectives of the Government.

9.1.2 Ministry of Coal: Under the administrative control of the Ministry, key functions are performed such as determining policies and strategies in respect of exploration and development of coal and lignite reserves, sanctioning of important projects of high value and for deciding all related issues. These are performed through public sector undertakings, namely Coal India Ltd. (CIL) and its 8 subsidiaries, and Neyveli Lignite Corporation (NLC). Other than CIL and NLC, the Ministry also has a joint venture with Government of Andhra Pradesh, viz. Singareni Collieries Company Limited (SCCL). Government of Andhra Pradesh holds 51 percent equity and the rest 49 percent equity is held by the Government of India.

The Department of Coal is responsible for development and exploitation of coal and lignite reserves in India. The subjects allocated to the Department—which include attached and subordinate or other organizations including PSUs concerned with their subjects—under the Government of India (Allocation of Business) Rules, 1961, as amended from time to time, are as follows:

1. Exploration and development of coking coal and non-coking coal and lignite deposits in India.
2. All matters relating to production, supply, distribution and prices of coal.
3. Development and operation of coal washeries other than those for which Department of Steel (ISPAT Vibhag) is responsible.
4. Low temperature carbonization of coal and production of synthetic oil from coal.
5. Administration of the Coal Mines (Conservation and Development) Act, 1974.
6. Coal Mines Provident Fund Organization.
7. Coal Mines Welfare Organization.

8. Administration of the Coal Mines Provident Fund and Miscellaneous Provision Act, 1948.
9. Administration of the Coal Mines Labour Welfare Fund Act, 1947.
10. Rules under the Mines Act, 1952 for the levy and collection of duty of excise on coke and coal produced and dispatched from mines and administration of rescue fund.
11. Administration of the Coal Bearing Areas (Acquisition and Development) Act, 1957.
12. Administration of the Mines and Minerals (Development and Regulation) Act, 1957 and other Union Laws in so far the said Act and Laws relate to coal and lignite and sand for stowing, business incidental to such administration including questions concerning various States.

9.1.3 Ministry of Petroleum and Natural Gas: Petroleum is a Central subject vide Entry 53 in List I (Union List) of the Seventh Schedule of the Constitution of India. It reads, "Regulation and development of oil fields and mineral oil resources, petroleum and petroleum products, other liquids and substances declared by Parliament to be dangerously inflammable".

The Ministry of Petroleum and Natural Gas, Government of India, is entrusted with the responsibility of exploration and production of oil and natural gas, their refining, distribution and marketing, import, export, and conservation.

In the wake of the ongoing liberalisation programme, the petroleum industry (both upstream and the downstream) has been thrown open to private sector participation (both Indian and foreign). The response, particularly in the downstream sector, has been encouraging.

A New Exploration Licensing Policy (NELP) with certain fiscal and financial incentives has been announced recently to boost investment in exploration.

This could help in accretion of the hydrocarbon reserves. NELP has met with some success in finding gas in the country and in offshore areas.

9.1.4 Ministry of New and Renewable Energy (MNRE): The role of new and renewable energy has been assuming increasing significance in recent times with the growing concern for the country's energy security. Energy self-sufficiency was identified as the major driver for new and renewable energy in the country in the wake of the two oil shocks of the 1970s.

MNRE is responsible mainly for research and development, intellectual property protection, and international cooperation, promotion, and coordination in renewable energy sources such as wind power, small hydro, biogas, and solar power. The broad aim of MNRE is to develop and deploy new and renewable energy for supplementing the energy requirements of the country.

9.1.5 Department of Atomic Energy (DAE): DAE is directly under the Prime Minister of India with headquarters in Mumbai. The department is responsible for nuclear technology, including nuclear power and research.

Nuclear power for civil use is well established in India. Its civil nuclear strategy has been directed towards complete independence in the nuclear fuel cycle necessary because it is excluded from the 1970 Nuclear Non-Proliferation Treaty (NPT) due to its acquiring nuclear weapons capability after 1970. As a result, India's nuclear power programme has proceeded largely without fuel or technological assistance from other countries.

9.2 Electricity Policy Reforms and Private Sector

Rapid economic growth cannot be realised if energy is not available at reasonable costs. Electricity is a crucial energy input in this context.

Power sector reforms were initiated in 1991 to encourage competition in each sub-element of the sector, namely generation, transmission and distribution under an independent and transparent regulatory regime. With this objective in mind a Central Electricity Regulatory Commission (CERC) was set up at the national level and State Electricity Regulatory Commissions (SERCs) were set up at the level of States. Private sector participation was also set in motion with the enactment of the Electricity Laws (Amendment) Act in 1998. The Government of India has taken a number of measures, in consultation with State Governments and other stakeholders, to improve power situation in the country.

9.2.1 Electricity Act, 2003: Electricity Act, 2003 replaced the three laws relating to electricity: Indian Electricity Act, 1910, Electricity (Supply) Act, 1948 and Electricity Regulatory Commission Act, 1998. Electricity Act, 2003 recognizes trading of power as a distinct activity and permits State Electricity Regulatory Commissions (SERCs) to allow open access in distribution of electricity in phases that would ultimately encourage efficiency and competition. The Act was enacted with the main objectives of providing a liberal and progressive framework for growth of power sector by introducing competition in different segments of generation, trading and distribution of electricity. It has removed barriers to entry of private sectors in these segments.

This new legislation brings into effect many measures to ensure protection of consumers in terms of quality of service, price regulation, right to get service on demand and redressal of grievances. The Act also provides appropriate institutional mechanisms for achieving the goal of supply of electricity to all areas. It also lays down the framework for reorganization of the State Electricity Boards (SEBs) in a time frame to be decided by the State Government with consent of the Central Government.

Under the new statutory regime, generation of power is completely de-licensed and captive power generation is freely allowed. It allows open access to transmission network under regulatory supervision. Any generating company is now free to seek distribution license and vice versa. The present opaque cross subsidies would be slowly phased out, and replaced by a transparent and explicit subsidy to meet the social objectives prioritized by the State Government. For rural and inaccessible areas, stand alone systems involving generation and distribution are allowed without the requirement of license, and decentralized system of local distribution would be allowed through panchayats, user associations, co-operatives or franchises. In this liberalized framework, multiple players in generation, supply and trading will compete in the marketplace under the oversight of the regulator.

An important innovation of Electricity Act, 2003 is the statutory provision for open access which allows generating stations to enter the market and sell directly to high tension consumers. They can do so through assured access to the grid to reach such consumers while paying the distribution company a reasonable wheeling charge and a surcharge in lieu of the cross subsidy element. Unfortunately, most regulators have fixed the surcharge at a very high level. It needs to be clarified that the surcharge is meant only to cover the legitimate loss of cross subsidy from high tariff paying consumers who may migrate to competing suppliers. It should not be set so high as to kill competition nor so low as to leave uncovered subsidy cross burden on the distribution utilities.

A. Electricity Rules, 2005: These rules were notified on June 8, 2005, which, among other things, describe the requirements for captive generating plants. These rules have provided clarity for the successful implementation of the provisions of Electricity Act, 2003.

9.2.2 Captive Power Generation: The Electricity Act, 2003 does away with the requirement of approval/clearance of any authority for setting up a captive generating plant. The new law (as amended) also ensures non-discriminatory open access for transmission of electricity generated from a captive generating plant to the destination of its use, subject to availability of transmission capacity. The surcharge and cross subsidies are being progressively reduced in a manner as may be specified by the State Regulatory Commission. Any person setting up a captive power plant can also establish and maintain dedicated transmission lines.

The industrial sector is the largest consumer of electricity. Besides purchasing power from the utilities, a number of industries, viz. aluminium, cement, fertilizer, iron, steel, paper, sugar etc. have their own captive power plants either to supplement the electricity supply from the utilities or for generating electricity as a by-product through co-generation. Captive power plants are being set up by industries to meet their own power requirements to enable them to tide over problems due to power shortages and poor quality of supply.

In accordance with the guidelines issued by the Ministry of Power, the following categories are eligible to install captive power plants:

1. A consumer of electricity.
2. A group comprising more than one consumer as a joint venture.
3. An actual user of power but not a consumer.
4. A group of actual users of power, but not consumers, as a joint venture.
5. If the captive plant falls under the category of hydro or co-generation plant, such plant may be permitted, irrespective of its size and the power supply position in the state.
6. If the captive power plant is based on coal or liquid fuel or gas and if the state is deficit in power supply, the installation of the plant could normally be allowed and the plant can be permitted to have a capacity up to 200 percent of the requirement of the host industry.
7. If the captive power plant is based on coal, liquid fuel or gas and the state is surplus in power, the installation of such captive plants can still be considered in cases where the state/SEB cannot guarantee uninterrupted supply or stipulated quality of supply (within prescribed voltage and frequency variations) required by the industry or a particular process. Further, captive generation may also be permitted if it is found, after a review of costs and tariffs, to be more economical than grid supply.

8. Banking facilities may also be provided to the captive plants so that available capacities are utilized to the extent possible and when required. The rates for banking may be determined on mutually agreed terms.
9. Units in special economic zones (SEZs) and industrial estates may be allowed to set up captive power plants liberally.

9.2.3 Trading in Electricity: A major consequence of the Electricity Act, 2003 is a rise in trading in electricity. The Central Electricity Regulatory Commission (CERC) has implemented a key provision of the Act, and by issuing regulations for open access in inter-state transmission, heralded a new chapter in the electricity sector. The open access regulations enable generation companies, distribution companies, electricity traders and captive plant owners to access transmission networks across the country for the purpose of transporting electricity.

The CERC has implemented availability based tariff (ABT) in all the 5 electrical regions of the country at the inter-state level. The ABT facilitates merit order dispatch of various generating stations having different variable costs. The ABT has the unique feature of flexibility to cater to fluctuations in demand of power in the electricity grid through a commercial pricing mechanism known as the unscheduled energy inter-change rate (UI rate). The price for unscheduled inter-changes of energy is related to grid frequency in a manner to encourage grid discipline. As a result, the gird frequency has improved remarkably after the implementation of ABT in the country. The UI mechanism facilitates the spot sale or purchase of electricity into or out of the electricity grid and does not require the services of a trader. As UI mechanism is an alternative to formal trading, it provides a sort of benchmark price for trading of electricity and does not allow the price of traded electricity to shoot up.

These developments take the market for electricity closer to other normal markets in the economy, such as markets for garments or footwear, in that there is competition between multiple producers, and customers have choices. CERC is the regulator and licensing authority for firms that seek to engage in power trading. CERC issued regulations governing licensing for power trading in January 2004.

Power Trading Corporation (PTC) and Vidyut Vyapar Nigam (of NTPC) are important players in this nascent area. The creation of inter-regional link lines of nearly 4,300 MW capacity and online information available through 5 regional load dispatch centres (RLDCs), have also played a part.

As is the case with markets for other products, an extensive growth of trading will lead to a better utilization of the country's energy production. Liquid and efficient markets for electricity will tend to link up the marginal unit of electricity generated at some location in the country, to a consumer located elsewhere in the country with the highest incremental output from this electricity.

A highly beneficial aspect of this new paradigm is the onset of price flexibility, i.e. the commencement of *price volatility.* Fluctuations in price in this market for electricity are required, to induce rational responses on the part of producers and consumers. For example, when electricity prices are high, a supply response would be induced in the form of captive plant owners switching on their generation equipment in order to sell to consumers, and a demand response would be induced in the form of reduced consumption. These dynamic responses were stifled in the erstwhile policy framework, where the policy framework prevented volatility in the price of electricity. This marks a milestone in the steady progress that has been made in India in moving towards price flexibility in the full range of markets.

A logical extension of the spot market for electricity is market for future and options on electricity, which will allow buyers and sellers to make contracts governing future dates, and to do risk management. These markets exist in several countries abroad. There is a possibility of some kinds of electricity derivatives coming about in India in the near future.

9.2.4 Private Enterprise in Power Sector: On April 17, 1990, the Energy Minister announced in Parliament the relaxation of certain restrictions to encourage private sector participation in power generation schemes. It may be noted that power generation and distribution was reserved exclusively for the public sector in the Industrial Policy Resolution, 1956. The decision to open up the power sector, generation as well as distribution, to private companies was attributed to the perennial shortage of power and the inability of public sector units to meet the power requirements of the growing economy. Allowing private enterprises in power sector also showed Government's indignation with the poor performance of State Electricity Boards (SEBs) which have been incurring mounting losses.

A. Initiatives to Attract Private Investments: The present policy of the Government seeks to attract significant private sector investment in the Indian power sector. The key initiatives in this regard are the following:

1. Private sector has been permitted to set up coal, gas or liquid-based thermal projects, hydro projects and wind or solar projects of any size.
2. Foreign equity participation has been brought under automatic approval route for generation, transmission and distribution of power generation in hydro-electric, oil-based and coal/lignite-based power projects.
3. Role of the Central Government has been curtailed and the State Governments and State Electricity Boards (SEBs) have been empowered to negotiate directly with developers, facilitating speedy clearances for the investors.
4. Ancillary sector such as coal has been significantly deregulated. 100 percent foreign equity is permitted.
5. State Governments have agreed to allow the gradual entry of the private sector in distribution.

Government recognizes the fact that private investors have important role to play in the power sector growth map of India.

The stipulation under Section 63 of Electricity Act, 2003 has provided impetus to the participation of private sector in generation and transmission. Provision of open access and tariff framework under tariff policy has been put in place to create an enabling environment for the private investors.

Under the Electricity Act, 2003, non-discriminatory open access in transmission and distribution has been envisaged. The move is intended to encourage competition amongst generators and distributors and trading in power from surplus to deficit regions.

Section 14 of the Electricity Act, 2003 allows any generator of electricity to distribute electricity in a rural area without the requirement of any license, subject to compliance with the measures as may be specified by the Central Electricity Authority (CEA) under Section 53. Under the provisions of Section 4 of the Act, the Central Government, in consultation with the State Governments, prepared and notified Rural Electrification Policy in 2006, facilitating stand alone systems (including those based on renewable sources of energy and other non-conventional sources of energy) for rural areas.

B. Foreign Direct Investment (FDI) in the Power Sector: The Government has announced significant new policy initiatives to attract foreign investment in this sector.

In exploration and production, oil and gas fields are open to the private sector as well as for foreign participation under production sharing contracts. Foreign investment in it is permitted up to 100 percent in small-sized oil fields; 60 percent for unincorporated joint ventures and 51 percent for incorporated joint ventures; and 100 percent for exploration and production of blocks identified under the new Exploration Licensing Policy.

The level of FDI in oil refining sector under automatic approval has been raised from 49 percent to 100 percent. For gas fields developed in the private sector, promoters are free to market the gas at market-related prices.

FDI is permitted up to 74 percent in infrastructure related to marketing of petroleum products.

As per the new policy, foreign investors can enter into a joint venture with an Indian partner for financial and/or technical collaboration and also for setting up of renewable energy based power generation projects. The liberalised foreign investment approval regime aims at facilitating foreign investment and transfer of technology through joint ventures. Government of India is encouraging foreign investors to set up renewable energy based power generation project on build-own-operate basis.

9.3 Coal Mining

Coal resources in India are unevenly distributed and have high ash content. While coal is needed all over the country, production is concentrated in the States of Jharkhand, Odisha, Chhattisgarh, West Bengal, Madhya Pradesh, Andhra Pradesh and Maharashtra. Therefore, coal has to be carried over long distances, resulting in burden on the transport infrastructure, particularly railways.

9.3.1 Private Sector Participation in Coal Mining: Private sector participation in coal mines has been allowed in recent years to fill the gap between coal demand and production.

Following the economic reforms initiated in 1991, the private sector has been allowed to mine coal for captive consumption under the Captive Mining Policy, 1993. The captive mining policy allows allocation of blocks to designated end-users for mining coal for their own use. The current list of authorized end-users includes power, steel and cement producers. FDI has been permitted in coal mining, and joint ventures are also permitted. A large number of coal blocks stand allocated to private entrepreneurs for developing captive mines but only few of these mines have started production. The captive mining policy has significant hurdles and has not been a success so far, either in raising domestic production or in increasing the number of domestic producers.

It is imperative to bring in necessary legislative changes to the existing legal framework to facilitate private sector participation in coal production and distribution. Measures are needed to further streamline the administrative procedures to expedite the necessary clearances and required legislative changes. The role of private sector at present is limited to the extent of allocating captive mines for power generation, steel plants and for cement making. Private participation should be encouraged in coal mining in the years to come. Regulatory mechanism will have to be created to ensure proper and systematic development and exploitation of coal mines, and appropriate pricing of different grades of coal so that the consumers benefit and greater competition is encouraged. A proper evaluation of recoverable reserves is also important for the purpose of fixing of royalty, the basis of which should not be the quantity of coal actually mined but the recoverable reserves.

In order to attract private investment, financial incentives and concessions—as applicable to infrastructure sectors like power and telecommunications—need to be extended to this sector. This would facilitate increased market borrowings and easy access to capital markets. The project cost would also come down as a result of lower import duties on plant and machinery which form the major part of project cost.

Privatisation of the existing coal mines also needs to be considered. A start can be made with the privatisation of mines which are presently fully linked to a limited number of users. The concept can then be extended to other mines which are more merchant in nature.

9.3.2 Auctioning of Coal Blocks: Prime Minister Narendra Modi announced on May 12, 2020 the Aatmanirbhar Bharat Abhiyan which combined relief, policy reforms and fiscal and monetary measures to help businesses and individuals to cope with the situation created by Covid-19 pandemic. A mega package of ₹ 20 lakh crore (10 percent of GDP) was announced for the purpose. The details of the ₹ 20 lakh crore package were announced by Finance Minister

Nirmala Sitharaman in five tranches during the next five consecutive days.

The fourth tranche, announced on May 16, 2020, related to measures which included a major opening up of coal, defence production, civil aviation, power, space, social infrastructure and atomic energy for private participation.

The government started auctioning coal blocks for commercial mining from June 18, 2020. This move will finally free the sector from government controls, unlock its potential to substitute imports and fuel growth.

9.4 Private Players in Petroleum and Natural Gas

The liberalisation and globalization processes started in 1991 have thrown up many opportunities and challenges for the petroleum and natural gas sector in India. To increase domestic production of crude oil and natural gas, NELP was launched in 1997-98. At the end of 7 rounds of NELP bidding in 2007, 256 blocks were offered. The 8th and 9th rounds of bidding have awarded 32 and 14 exploration blocks in 2010 and 2012 respectively. The acquisition of equity oil and gas abroad in a number of countries is also being pursued by both PSUs and private sector companies.

In order to meet the shortfall in the demand for natural gas, imports from Iran, Myanmar and Central Asian countries through trans-national pipelines are being pursued. The import of gas in the form of liquefied natural gas (LNG) started at Dahej LNG terminal in 2005.

With a view to create competition, new entrants are being allowed since March 2002 to market transportation fuels, namely motor spirit, high speed diesel and aviation turbine fuel. The Government has issued retail licenses to Reliance Industries, Essar Oil, Shell, ONGC, Mangalore Refineries and Petrochemicals Limited and the Numaligarh Refinery.

Lately, the Government has taken a number of steps to control and regulate the volatility in petroleum prices and augment production of oil and natural gas. Petroleum and Natural Gas Regulatory Act, 2006 was notified on April 3,

2006 to regulate specific activities relating to petroleum, petroleum products and natural gas consequent to deregulation of the petroleum sector.

The petroleum sector dominates India's current energy use. This is one of the most vulnerable sectors in the Indian energy scenario. As an oil deficit country, India is dependent upon imports of the crude oil from West Asian countries. India imports oil from 28 countries, though five countries—Nigeria, Saudi Arabia, UAE, Kuwait and Iran—account for more than 75 percent of the total oil imports. The Persian Gulf region alone supplies more than 67 percent of India's needs.

10

Railways, Roads, Shipping and Civil Aviation

Transport sectors such as railways, roads, ports and airports are crucial for the growth of the economy due to their multiplier effects. Immense pressure on existing transport infrastructure due to rapid urbanization and expanding trade has had a negative multiplier effect on the economy, hampering trade, efficient logistics, connectivity and business operations. Thus, reviving and building a world-class transport infrastructure are among the top priorities on the current government's development agenda.

Clearly, there is an urgent call to action from the Government to address the growing requirements and constantly monitor the status of ongoing PPP activity in key transport sectors. This will also help ensure that the Government's operating environment is adapting fast enough to the evolving needs of the private sector.

Transport is the dominant PPP sector in India both by number of projects and investments, mainly due to the large number of road sector projects.

Government has taken a slew of measures to revitalize the PPP model to attract private investment like introducing the hybrid annuity model (HAM) and toll-operate-transfer (TOT) in the road sector, Sagarmala Programme for port-led development, Station Redevelopment Programme in railways sector and the recently launched Regional Connectivity Scheme (RCS) in the civil aviation sector.

Some noteworthy events that have happened during the recent past include adoption of new PPP modalities in the roads sector, permission to infuse funds in languishing projects, liberalization of exit policies, creation of the Rail Development Authority and non-fare revenue directorate in railways, and monetization of assets through station redevelopment programs and the toll-operate-transfer (TOT) model.

10.1 Indian Railways

Railways are an important part of India's transport infrastructure and it has much higher fuel efficiency than trucks and cars in terms of fuel consumption per tonne kilometre or per passenger kilometre. For movement of bulk commodities, trucks cannot compete with railways. With containerisation, railways can be competitive even for movement of other goods over long distance.

Railways, without doubt, are among the main foundations on which the national economy rests. It provides a service which is safe, economical and efficient. In its operations, railways have always to keep abreast of modem scientific and technological developments. Diesel and electric motive power, improved designs of wagons and coaches and improved signalling and telecommunication equipment have to be employed to an increasing extent in order to secure economy and efficiency. Improvements along these lines should lead to the operation of longer, heavier and, to the extent necessary, faster trains, thus securing fuller use of line capacity and rolling stock.

10.1.1 Public-Private-Partnership (PPP): Private sector participation in container movement is already unfolding on a large scale after it was decided to introduce competition in this segment. Necessary MCA has been finalized, agreements signed with 15 parties in January 2007, and the scheme has since been operationalised with seven new operators, excluding CONCOR, commencing operations by utilizing about 30 new rakes.

This policy is required to be taken forward by building in suitable guarantees and commitments from railways in order to enable the private operator to provide value added container services and make investments in container handling facilities like ICDs and container freight stations (CFSs). Long-term commitments on transit time and access charges on the part of

Railways would be necessary for stimulating private investments in the container logistics sector.

A range of PPP models have been identified which need further fine tuning. These include multimodal logistics parks, upgradation of major freight and passenger terminal, construction of road over bridges, Railway OFC network, consolidation of piece meal parcels into wagons and train loads etc. A programme for redevelopment of 22 railway stations into world class stations through PPPs has already been initiated.

10.1.2 Private Sector Participation: The participation of both private and public sectors in developing rail infrastructure has gone up. A joint venture company was formed with Pipava Port authorities to provide broad gauge connectivity to Pipava Port. MoUs have been signed between Ministry of Railways and the State Governments of Andhra Pradesh, Karnataka, Maharashtra, West Bengal, Tamil Nadu and Jharkhand in developing rail infrastructure in these States.

Ministry of Railways policy on rail connectivity and capacity augmentation projects of December 2012 has encouraged participation of the private sector in providing last mile connectivity to ports, large mines, cluster of industries for building rail connectivity and capacity augmentation. The policy had proposed the following five models:

1. Non-government private line model.
2. Joint ventures.
3. Capacity augmentation through funding by customers.
4. BOT.
5. Capacity augmentation through annuity model.

The first three models involve participation of strategic investors/customers and leverage the requirement of such investors and railways for having last mile connectivity. The other two-models are pure PPP models. All the models provide a clear revenue stream to the investor for making the connectivity projects bankable. Three Model Concession Agreements for private line model, joint venture and BOT have been approved and put in public domain. The agreements for the other two models are under approval process.

These agreements have tried to balance the risk allocations between private and public sector. Under this policy, rail connectivity to Dhamra Port has been commissioned. Projects of rail connectivity to Tuna Port, Jaigarh Port and coal connectivity projects in Chhattisgarh are under implementation apart from four projects under customer funded model. Seven projects have been given i*n principle* approval by MoR.

Though efforts have been made to involve private sector in creation of rail infrastructure, but this has been met with limited success. Absence of regulatory mechanism, no control over network and tariff, uncertainty of traffic materialization and delay in processes has not generated confidence among the investors. Railways would be required to lay down certain benchmarks for appraisal which would be acceptable to the market to enable the relevant projects to be financed.

10.1.3 Foreign Direct Investment (FDI): Vide Notification No. S.O.2113(E) dated August 22, 2014, Government of India has opened up the following activities of Indian railways for FDI.

Construction, operation, maintenance of:

1. Suburban corridor projects through PPP.
2. High speed train projects.
3. Dedicated freight lines.
4. Rolling stock including train sets, and locomotives or coach manufacturing and maintenance facilities.
5. Railway electrification.
6. Signalling systems.
7. Freight terminals.
8. Passenger terminals.
9. Infrastructure in industrial park pertaining to railway lines or sidings including electrified railway lines and connectivity to main railway lines.
10. Mass rapid transport systems.

Detailed Sectoral Guidelines on FDI have been issued which provide permissible areas and conditions of engagement. As against debt, FDI involves investment in equity which involves greater risk for the investor vis-à-vis debt and, therefore, also expectation of higher returns. Considering the positive BOT agreement, investment should flow in these projects as and when they are launched. An investors' meet was organized on December 5, 2014, wherein a booklet on "Overview of Framework for Participative Models of Rail Connectivity and Domestic and Foreign Direct Investment" was released. In this booklet, projects have been identified for domestic/foreign direct investments in Railways.

10.1.4 High Speed Train Project: The Japan International Co-operation Agency (JICA) which undertook the study on the feasibility of this prestigious project, submitted its report in July 2015. The project was approved by the Cabinet Committee on Economic Affairs in December 2015, to be implemented with Japanese technical and financial assistance. The memorandum of understanding for co-operation between India and Japan was signed on December 12, 2015. A new special purpose vehicle with 50 percent equity participation from the Ministry of Railways and 50 percent from the State Governments of Maharashtra and Gujarat is to be set up to implement the project.

A. Salient Features of the Project: These are as under:

1. Total construction cost of the project is approximately ₹ 70,915 crore including land cost. Project completion cost is approximately ₹ 97,636 crore (including price escalation, interest during construction and import duties). Average per kilometre cost of construction works out to be ₹ 140 crore.
2. Project implementation time will be approximately 7 years from the commencement of construction.
3. Japanese official development assistance will be ₹ 79,165 crore (81 percent of project cost) for 50 years with 0.1 percent interest rate and a 15-year moratorium.
4. Certain identified packages would have either a Japanese company as prime contractor or a Japanese-led JV.
5. Certain identified goods manufactured in Japan would be procured from Japan.

6. Total length of the proposed corridor will be 508 kilometres between the Bandra Kurla complex in Mumbai and Sabarmati/Ahmedabad in Gujarat.
7. Sixty-four percent of the corridor will be constructed on embankment, 25 percent via duct and 6 percent tunnel, with a standard gauge.
8. The stretch will cover 12 stations between Mumbai and Sabarmati.
9. The maximum design speed will be 350 kmph with an operating speed of 320 kmph.
10. It will have 10-car trains (750 seats) in the beginning and 16-car trains (1,200 seats) in the future.
11. Thirty-five trains per day each way will operate by 2023, which will go up to 105 trains per day each way in 2053.
12. It will have approximately 36,000 daily users per day (both ways) in 2023, i.e. 13 million per annum projected, which will go up to 1,86,000 per day (both ways) or 68 million per annum by 2053.

10.1.5 Redevelopment and Modernization of Railway Stations on PPP Mode: Indian Railways, in its quest to enhance customer experience by adding world-class passenger amenities, has launched a station redevelopment programme. The Government plans to leverage commercial development of land and air space in and around the station. The revenues realized from real estate development and commercials at station shall be utilized for station redevelopment and maintenance obligations.

Indian Railways holds great importance in development and growth of Indian economy as it provides connectivity to remote regions by providing affordable transport services to a large population and facilitates industrial and economic development through transport materials such as coal, iron ore, fertilizers and food grains.

The report of Expert Committee on Modernization of Indian Railways (Chairman: Sam Pitrodia) released in February 2012 had laid heavy emphasis on involvement of private sector in modernization activities. The report had identified key areas which would need to be taken up under PPP mode. The list of the key areas is as below:

1. Stations and terminals.
2. High speed rail corridors.
3. Elevated rail corridors.
4. Private freight terminals.
5. Leasing wagons.
6. Loco and coach manufacturing units.
7. Captive power generation.
8. Renewable energy projects.
9. Railway hospitals and schools.

10.2 Roads and Road Transport

Roads are the key to the development of an economy. A good road network constitutes the basic infrastructure that propels the development process through connectivity and opening up the backward regions to trade and investment. Roads also play a key role in inter-modal transport development, establishing links with airports, railway stations and ports. In addition, they have an important role in promoting national integration, which is particularly important in a large country like India.

10.2.2 Public-Private-Partnership (PPP): Historically, investments in infrastructure, particularly in the highways, were being made by the Government mainly because of the large volume of resources required, long gestation period, uncertain return and associated externalities. The galloping resource requirements and the concern for managerial efficiency and consumer responsiveness in recent times have led to an active involvement by the private sector also.

To encourage participation of the private sector, the Department of Road Transport and Highways has laid down comprehensive policy guidelines for private sector participation in the highway sector. Government has also announced several incentives such as tax exemptions and duty-free import of road building equipments and machinery to encourage private sector participation. It has been decided that all the sub-projects in National Highways Development Project (NHDP) Phase-III to Phase-VII would be taken up on the basis of PPP on build-operate-transfer (BOT) mode. The private sector participation envisaged in Phase-II of NHDP has also been increased.

Although, efforts have been made by several States to encourage and attract private sector financing in augmenting capacity of roads and provision of bridges, and bypasses, resources have remained a major constraint in the execution of the programmes for state roads. Other constraints include, inter alia, the following:

1. **Thin Spreading of Resources:** More projects are sanctioned than can be undertaken within the available resources, leading to spreading of available funds thinly and resulting in time and cost overruns.
2. **Delay in Pre-construction Activities:** Works have at times been awarded without acquiring full land for the project. This has affected obtaining the environmental clearance and shifting/removal of utilities.
3. **Weak Management by Contractors:** Although, several measures have been taken by the contracting industry to acquire state-of-art equipment and procure good technical and managerial staff, considerable scope exists for improvement in achieving project management excellence, proper scheduling of human resources and equipment resources.
4. **Poor Implementation Capacities:** The State PWDs are required to be reoriented for the current needs of modern technology and commercial management principles. There is a need to improve the capacity for planning, designing and execution of works to meet the transport demand of users in many States. Considerable scope also exists for enhancing the training arrangements of engineering personnel. Side by side contracting industry and consultancy sector also need to grow on healthy lines.

Almost all State governments have facilitated entry of private sector in providing passenger transport services to ease pressure on the public sector. Private bus operators have, however, exhibited deplorable quality of service, with disregard to traffic rules, unsafe driving practices, unscheduled operation, and usage of irrational cost cutting measures and tax evasion. The private sector has also adversely affected the performance of public sector by resorting to unfair competition.

A prerequisite is, therefore, to strictly enforce rules, for which specially designated regulatory bodies need to be set up, with powers to lay down minimum basic service standards, impose heavy fines, suspend or even cancel licenses, and launch and pursue vigorously prosecutions for accidents.

It is obvious that the provision of such a large network would need participation not only of the government agencies but also the private sector. For mobilising resources, dedicated levies and user charges will have to be imposed. Tolls can be charged on high density traffic corridors and the major bridges. The revenue thus earned should be spent on the development and maintenance of roads and provision of highway amenities. For encouraging private sector participation, various tax concessions have been offered. These need to be carried further. Consideration also needs to be given to the use of land development as a method of improving the viability of private investment in the road sector. For this, legislative changes may be necessary, particularly at the State-level.

10.3 Ports and Shipping

Maritime transport is a critical infrastructure for the economic development of a country. It influences the pace, structure and pattern of development. The maritime sector in India comprises of ports, overseas shipping, coastal shipping, inland water transport, shipbuilding and ship repair, ship breaking, maritime training, and international co-operation in maritime.

Ports and shipping are the backbone of the Exports and

Imports (EXIM) trade in India. India has a coastline that is more than 7,500 kilometres long, interspersed with more than 200 ports. Most cargo ships that sail between East Asia and America, and Europe and Africa pass through Indian territorial waters.

10.3.1 Private Sector Participation: Recent policy measures have ushered in new institutional arrangements and have yielded results in terms of measurable outcomes such as the delays at ports. While performance metrics have improved considerably, they continue to lag international standards. Private investment in the sector has been mainly from captive users, and these port terminals now compare well with international norms at efficiency.

For the purpose of attracting private sector investment, model bid documents have been prepared laying down transparent bidding procedure, including qualifications and selection criteria.

Traditionally, all over the world, the ownership of ports has been dominated by the public sector. But privatization of port facilities and services has now gathered momentum and India is also following the trend and an enabling policy framework has already been put in place. Depending on the nature of facility/service, private operators can enter into a service contract, a management contract, a concession agreement or a divestiture to operate port services. Areas that have been opened up to the private sector on a BOT basis include construction of cargo handling berths and dry-docks, container terminals and warehousing facilities and ship repair facilities.

The broad objectives of the participation of private sector in port development have been to bring about an improvement in efficiency, productivity, quality of service as well as to usher competitiveness in the provision of port services. In addition, the private sector is expected to mobilize adequate resources required for capacity augmentation and introduce the latest technology and management techniques in the port sector.

The Government has identified the following areas for

private sector participation:

1. Leasing out assets of the ports.
2. Construction and operation of container terminals, multiple cargo berths and specialized cargo berths, warehousing, storage facilities, tank farms, container freight stations, setting up of captive power plants etc.
3. Leasing of equipment for cargo handling and leasing of floating rafts from the private sector.
4. Pilotage.
5. Captive facilities for port based industries.

10.3.2 Joint Ventures: The objective of setting up joint ventures is to attract new technology, introduce better managerial practices, implementation of schemes, foster strategic alliances with minor ports for the creation of optimal port infrastructure and enhance the confidence levels of the private sector in funding the ports.

A scheme for joint ventures between major port and foreign ports, between major port and minor ports, without tender, as well as major port and companies following the tender route was approved by the Cabinet and guidelines on joint venture formation were issued. Amendments to the Major Port Trusts Act, 1963 for this purpose came into effect from September 1, 2000.

10.4 Civil Aviation

Air transport worldwide is the preferred mode of transport especially for long distance travel, business travel, accessing difficult terrains and for transporting high value and perishable commodities mainly on account of the speed of travel and saving of time. With the opening up of domestic skies to private carriers, air services have become affordable and are now effectively competing with other modes of transport.

The main advantage of civil aviation vis-à-vis railways and road transport is the speed of travel and consequent saving of time. A part of this gain is, however, nullified for short-haul flights due to time taken in reporting, security checks, flying, luggage clearance etc. Air travel, nevertheless, retains a substantial edge over other modes of transport for long distance travel. It is particularly useful for business travel, international tourism and for transporting high value and perishable commodities. Air transport also provides easy accessibility to remote regions, which has implications for national integration and security. The advantage, however, has to be weighed against high cost of air travel and cost to the economy because of its high fuel intensity.

The civil aviation sector plays an important role in India's economy. It provides fast and reliable mode of transport across the country and is particularly important for many areas/places still not adequately connected by rail or road. With increasing globalization, this sector will play a more significant role in integrating the Indian economy with the rest of the world.

It is now increasingly recognized that aviation, far from being a mere mode of transportation for a small elite group, makes an important contribution to the national economy and is crucial for sustainable development of trade and tourism. The civil aviation sector has made significant strides in coping with the growth of international and domestic traffic. This sector provides three categories of services, viz. operational, infrastructure and regulatory-cum-developmental.

Until 2013, Airports Authority of India (AAI) was the only major player involved in developing and upgrading airports in India. Post-liberalization, private sector participation in the sector has been increasing. Currently, five international airports (Delhi, Mumbai, Cochin, Hyderabad, and Bengaluru) have been completed successfully under the PPP mode. These five airports together handle over 55 percent of the country's air traffic.

10.4.1 From Monopoly to Competition: The monopoly of public sector air carriers ended with the amendment of Air Corporation Act, 1953 in March 1994. Automatic approval for foreign equity participation in airport infrastructure up to 100 percent has been allowed. Foreign equity up to 40 percent and investment by non-resident Indians up to 100 percent is also permitted. Equity from foreign airlines is not allowed in domestic air-transport services directly or indirectly. Foreign financial institutions allowed to hold equity in the domestic air transport sector provided they do not have foreign airlines as their shareholders.

Foreign investors are allowed to have representation (up to 33 percent of total) on board of directors of the domestic airline company. Government is considering private sector participation, construction and operation of new airports on a BOT basis. The private sector is now playing a crucial role in the development of both airline and airport sector. The private sector share is likely to increase in the years to come.

The development of airports in the country is no longer in the domain of public sector. The Airport Infrastructure Policy, 1997, permits private equity participation in development of airport infrastructure. Success has been achieved in developing green-field airport in the country.

With the initiative of State Government of Kerala, a new international airport has been constructed and commissioned at Cochin. The project has been financed from contributions from non-resident Indians and loan from financial institutions. The airport is being managed by Cochin International Airport Ltd. in which the State Government holds majority shareholdings.

10.4.2 National Civil Aviation Policy (NCAP), 2016: Government released on June 15, 2016 the National Civil Aviation Policy, 2016. This was the first time since Independence in 1947 that an integrated civil aviation policy was brought out by the Government. The centre-piece of the policy is to make regional air connectivity a reality.

The policy aims to take flying to the masses by making it affordable and convenient, establish an integrated eco-system which will lead to significant growth of the civil aviation sector to promote tourism, employment and balanced regional growth, enhance regional connectivity through fiscal support and infrastructure development and enhance ease of doing business through deregulation, simplified procedures and e-governance.

10.4.3 Regional Connectivity Scheme (RCS) or UDAN (Ude Desh ka Aam Naagrik): The Ministry of Civil Aviation (MoCA), Government of India released the National Civil Aviation Policy (NCAP), 2016. One of the objectives of NCAP, 2016 is to "enhance regional connectivity through fiscal support and infrastructure development".

As the Indian economy grows, consumption-led growth in populated metros is expected to spill over to hinterland areas. This is also expected to be on account of factors of production (land, labour etc.) becoming costlier in the densely populated metro cities. In this scenario, air connectivity can provide required impetus to the economic growth of regional centres (towns/cities). In this context, one of the key objectives of NCAP, 2016 is to "establish an integrated eco-system which will lead to significant growth of civil aviation sector, which in turn would promote tourism, increase employment and lead to a balanced regional growth".

The operation of RCS is proposed to be through a market mechanism where operators will assess demand on routes; submit proposals for operating /providing connectivity on such route(s); seek viability gap funding (VGF), if any, while committing to certain minimum operating conditions; and the same shall be finalized in interaction with other market participants as provided for in this scheme.

The primary objective of RCS is to facilitate/stimulate regional air connectivity by making it affordable. Promoting affordability of regional air connectivity is envisioned under RCS by supporting airline operators through the following:

1. Concessions by Central Government, State Governments and airport operators to reduce the cost of airline operations on regional routes/other support measures.
2. Financial (viability gap funding or VGF) support to meet the gap, if any, between the cost of airline operations and expected revenues on such routes.

In short, RCS is one of the key elements of NCAP, 2016, which envisions domestic ticketing of 30 crore by 2022 and 50 crore by 2027. RCS as well as NCAP, 2016 would eventually promote growth of the entire civil aviation sector. RCS would lead to creation of regional air connectivity/services that would have spin-off benefits within the sector in terms of passengers taking other flights (not under RCS) and using airports/airport services that are not at concessional rates.

11

Telecommunications and Information Technology (IT)

Telecommunications is one of the prime support services needed for rapid growth and modernization of various sectors of the economy. It has become especially important in recent years because of enormous growth of information technology (IT) and its significant impact on the rest of the economy. India is perceived to have a special comparative advantage in IT and IT-enabled services. However, sustaining this advantage depends critically on high quality telecommunication infrastructure. Keeping this in view, the focus has to be on the provision of world class telecommunication facilities at reasonable rates.

11.1 Post-Independence Telecommunications Policy

Soon after Independence in 1947, the Government launched centralised planning process in the form of Five Year Plans. Resource allocation for the telecom sector was low and priority was given to sectors such as roads, power, sanitation, education, health etc. Till 1985, resource deployment in the telecom sector was around 2 to 3 percent of the total budget allocation. With no access to any other sources of funds, this sector registered low to moderate growth.

At the beginning of the Seventh Five Year Plan (1985-90), the Government decided to focus on improving this sector and constituted the Telecommunications Board and the Department of Telecommunications (DoT) within the Ministry of Communications to oversee operations, maintenance and development of telecom services (telecom was till then under the purview of the Posts and Telegraph Department within the Ministry of Communications). A new emphasis was also laid on the funding of the telecom sector. Whereas the plan budget of the Department of Telecom was still regulated by the central planning process and the Ministry of Finance, it was agreed in principle that additional resource mobilisation through market borrowing would be permitted in respect of the telecom sector.

11.1.1 Entry of Private Sector: In India, telecommunication sector was the monopoly of public sector till recently. Due to high cost and poor quality of services provided by public sector, it was recognised that capacities must expand much more rapidly and competition be introduced to improve the quality of service and encourage induction of new technology. Communications has become especially important in the context of enormous growth of information technology (IT) and its impact on rest of the economy. India is perceived to have a special comparative advantage in information technology/IT-enabled services, both of which depend critically on high quality communications infrastructure.

Following the Industrial Policy Statement in the Parliament on July 24, 1991, the telecom sector was opened up for private participation. As a result, the private telecom companies have started operations in the India due to vast availability of market potentials. Slowly, they have picked up their market share and currently they outperform the government-owned services due to increasing commercial gains.

Adoption of unified access service, accepting the intra-circle mergers and acquisitions, licensing regulations and announcement of broadband policy, the private sector has continued to play a significant role in the growth of the telecom sector and their participation has increased significantly during the recent period.

The Government continues to provide incentives to the telecom sector and reduced the license fees significantly. Due to acute competition in this sector, the tariffs for various services have experienced a downward movement apart from harmonization. New mobile phone connections have been increasing substantially during the recent period.

The private sector projects are reported to be working successfully in the cellular segment due to increase in commercial gains and also vast investment opportunities available in this sector. Though it appears to be a major success story in private sector participation in the telecom sector, some of the issues deserve attention. Issues such as spectrum allocation, tariff rationalization, etc., need to be addressed to encourage further healthy competition in this sector.

The telecommunication sector has witnessed a substantial growth rate since the initiation of economic reforms in 1991. Prior to this, the spread of telecommunication facilities on per capita basis was slow as compared to even other developing countries. Most of the rural areas did not have any means of telecommunication. This sector was characterised by near monopoly of the provision of services by the public sector. Even manufacturing of telecomm equipment was mainly in the hands of public sector till 1991. Since then, the manufacturing of telecom equipment has been deregulated. With the opening of the sector, the prices of some of the telecom equipments as well as provision of the services have declined. As a result, the telecom sector is likely to be one of the fastest growing sectors in the economy.

With the opening of international long distance services and internet telephony from April 2002, the process of liberalization and opening up the sector for competition was completed. Apart from opening up the basic as well as value-added market segment of telecom services to the private sector, the Government has taken major initiatives in offering a level playing field to operators by constituting the Telecom Regulatory Authority of India (TRAI). However, a great deal needs to be done, especially in terms of the implementation strategy so that the country can enjoy the benefits of the reforms.

11.2 National Digital Communications Policy (NDCP), 2018

NDCP, 2018 seeks to unlock the transformative power of digital communications networks to achieve the goal of digital empowerment and improved well-being of the people of India. It attempts to outline a set of goals, initiatives, strategies and intended policy outcomes. NDCP, 2018 aims to accomplish the following strategic objectives by 2022:

1. Provisioning of broadband for all.
2. Creating 4 million additional jobs in the digital communications sector.
3. Enhancing the contribution of the digital communications sector to 8 percent of India's GDP from 6 percent in 2017.
4. Propelling India to the top 50 nations in the ICT Development Index of ITU from 134 in 2017.
5. Enhancing India's contribution to global value chains.
6. Ensuring digital sovereignty.

In pursuit of accomplishing these objectives by year 2022, NDCP, 2018 envisages three Missions:

1. **Connect India:** Creating robust digital communications infrastructure to promote broadband for all as a tool for socio-economic development, while ensuring service quality and environmental sustainability.
2. **Propel India:** Enabling next generation technologies and services through investments, innovations and intellectual property rights (IPRs) generation

- to harness the power of emerging digital technologies, including 5G, AI, IoT, Cloud and Big Data.
- to enable provision of future ready products and services.
- to catalyze the fourth industrial revolution (Industry 4.0) by promoting investments, innovations and IPRs.

3. **Secure India:** Ensuring sovereignty, safety and security of digital communications to secure the interests of citizens and safeguard the digital sovereignty of India with a focus on ensuring individual autonomy and choice, data ownership, privacy and security; while recognizing data as a crucial economic resource

11.3 Telecom Infrastructure

To enable India's transition into a digital economy and

knowledge society large investment in infrastructure, both optical fibre cable and towers, for wireless transmission is required. The Government is committed to extending the reach of the mobile network to remote and rural villages with support from the Universal Services Obligation Fund (USOF). In addition, investments are being made to lay optical fibre cable for high speed broadband connectivity in rural areas.

11.3.1 BharatNet: The Government is implementing the flagship BharatNet project (in phases), to link each of the 2.5 lakh gram panchayats of India through optical fibre network. This is the largest rural connectivity project of its kind in the world and is the first pillar of Digital India Programme. It will facilitate the delivery of various e-services and applications including e-health, e-education, e-governance and e-commerce in the future. The project envisages optimal mix of underground fibre, fibre over power lines, radio and satellite media for providing broadband connectivity which can be utilized by all categories of service providers on non-discriminatory basis.

11.3.2 Right of Way Rules: The Central Government has notified the Indian Telegraph Right of Way Rules, 2016 to regulate underground infrastructure (optical fibre) and over ground infrastructure (mobile towers). This rule is applicable to all telecom service providers holding a licence issued under sub-section (1) of Section 4 of the Indian Telegraph Act, 1885. These rules have simplified the grant of right of way permissions for creation of telecom infrastructure by making it transparent and time-bound.

Under the new Rules, applications for laying fibre underground cable as well as for setting up telecom towers have to be accepted or rejected within a period of 60 days failing which application will be deemed to have been approved. All Government agencies and municipal bodies will also have to establish an electronic interface to receive and process Right of Way permission within 1 year from coming into force of these Rules in November 2016. Further, telecom infrastructure cannot be shut down without following due process. This measure is expected to facilitate an increase in the pace of creation of infrastructure both in both rural and urban areas.

11.3.3 Telecom Spectrum: A major achievement in the sector has been bringing in transparency in the allocation of spectrum by adopting an auction process. This has also resulted in the highest ever upfront payment to the Government. There has been a marked thrust on improving efficiency in the use of spectrum by allowing spectrum sharing, trading and harmonisation.

A. Spectrum Sharing: Radio frequency spectrum is a scarce and finite resource and, therefore, its efficient utilisation is critical to the success of the telecom industry. Keeping in view the industry requirements, a number of initiatives have been taken in this direction.

Spectrum sharing was allowed for the first time in India on April 21, 2016 when operators were allowed to pool their respective spectrum holdings for using the whole spectrum block (which was the sum of their respective holdings). Presently, spectrum is being shared by two service providers in 21 out of 22 service areas. Since spectrum efficiency increases exponentially with the size of the spectrum block, spectrum sharing has helped multiply spectrum efficiency many times without the need of additional spectrum, besides generating additional revenue for the Government.

B. Spectrum Trading: In another measure aimed at facilitating optimization of resources, the government has permitted trading of spectrum by allowing an access service provider (seller) to transfer spectrum usage rights and obligations to another access service provider (buyer). This is meant to facilitate optimisation of resources. The first such trade took place on May 17, 2016 and this facility has thereafter been utilised by a number of telecom service providers. Spectrum trading enables telecom players to sell their spectrum and exit leading to consolidation in the sector.

This has helped reduce the number of service providers from 10 to 8, thereby reducing fragmentation of spectrum. Trading also facilitates ease of doing business through greater competition, incentives for innovation, better/new services being available to consumers at cheaper tariffs

C. Spectrum Harmonisation: The high point of spectrum management has been the harmonisation of spectrum in 800 MHz and 1800 MHz bands that was carried out from April to September, 2016 resulting in rationalisation of spectrum holdings of telecom service providers, and transferring defence holdings to the defence bands. Consequentially, about 197 MHz of additional spectrum was recovered from its erstwhile use as guard and separation bands and was sold for more than ₹ 15,000 crore in the October 2016 auction. Harmonization of spectrum has helped improve quality of service by making fragmented frequency spots contiguous for efficient utilisation by service providers and making more spectrums available for the auction conducted in October 2016.

D. Spectrum Auction: India has suffered from a chronic shortage of spectrum. This was dealt with decisively through the mega auction of spectrum in 700, 800, 900, 1800, 2100, 2300 & 2500 MHz bands that was concluded successfully in October 2016. The auction sold 965 MHz of spectrum in different bands, which is more than 929 MHz sold cumulatively in last four auctions from 2012 to 2015. The auction also fetched a total amount of ₹ 66,000 crore, and highest ever upfront payment of ₹ 33,000 crore since 2012.

The auction of October 2016 was the most complex and sophisticated auction of natural resources and was conducted smoothly and transparently, without any glitch. The auction addressed the issue of spectrum scarcity in the country and call drops.

11.3.4 Harnessing Emerging Technologies: In order to ensure that India is on track to harness the benefits of emerging technologies, government has taken the following initiatives:

A. 5G Network: The fifth generation of mobile network

communication technology, known as 5G, holds the promise of applications with high social and economic value, leading to a *hyper-connected society* in which technology will play an even more important role in people's lives. 5G will not only facilitate but also add a new dimension to the missions like *Digital India* and *Smart Cities*. The Government envisages positioning India as a globally synchronized participant in the design, development and manufacturing of 5G-based technologies, products and applications.

Therefore, Government has constituted a multi-disciplinary High Level Forum to suggest vision, mission and goals for 5G India 2020 along with action plan and roadmap.

DoT is supporting research and study in 5G through financial assistance to institutions of national importance for establishment of Indigenous 5G Test Bed at IIT Chennai, in collaboration with premier technology institutions including IIT Delhi, IIT Mumbai, IIT Hyderabad and IISC Bengaluru.

B. M2M Communications: M2M represents tremendous opportunities in bringing substantial and tangible social and economic benefits to consumers, businesses, citizens and governments.

DoT intends to facilitate complete ecosystem around M2M networks in the backdrop of National Telecom M2M Roadmap which will act as the foundation for a digital society leading to integration of physical and digital infrastructure.

C. Transition to IPv6: Planned transition to Next Generation Internet Protocol, i.e. IPv6 assumes significance as it is essential for sustainable growth of internet, one of the key pillars of Digital India.

DoT, being the nodal department for IPv6 transition in the country, has been constantly working with all stakeholders including States, Union Territories (UTs), and Central Ministries/Departments for smooth transition to IPv6 since the release of National IPv6 Deployment Roadmap version-II in 2013 containing IPv6 transition guidelines/timelines.

11.3.5 Abolition of Wireless Operating License for Telecom Service Providers: To facilitate ease of doing business, DoT has abolished Wireless Operating License (WOL) for Access Service Providers from November 2, 2016. Earlier WOL was required for any transreceiver deployed in the telecom network by telecom service providers. This would obviate the need for endorsement by DoT and result in consequential convenience to telecom companies. Furthermore, this would prevent the delay in utilization of scarce infrastructure as radio transmission can be started immediately on installation of base stations without waiting for obtaining clearance from DoT.

11.3.6 Introduction of Virtual Network Operators (VNO): The Government issued guidelines for UL (VNO) on May 31, 2016. VNO system allows Telecom Service Providers to utilise their networks and spectrum efficiently by sharing active and passive infrastructure. Further, VNOs can provide services in small towns and rural areas using the network of existing TSPs having unutilised capacity or by last mile connectivity. This apart, the VNOs can be effective in providing services in airports or buildings or in smart cities. DoT has issued VNO licenses to 106 entities as on October 31, 2017.

11.3.7 Active Infrastructure Sharing: The Government issued a notification on February 11, 2016 permitting sharing of active infrastructure amongst service providers based on mutual agreements. The active sharing would cover antenna, feeder cable, Node B, Radio Access network (RAN) and transmission systems. This measure would help in provision of better and speedy services to the consumers while alleviating the cost burden incurred by the operators for laying telecom infrastructure.

11.4 Citizen and Customer-centric Measures

11.4.1 Full Mobile Number Portability (MNP): Government has allowed One Nation-Full Mobile Number Portability (MNP) recently. This has enabled the subscribers to change their licence service area and still retain their mobile number. MNP also allows subscribers to retain their existing mobile number when they switch from one telecom service provider to another irrespective of technology or service area limitation. This also helps in developing mobile numbers as an identity of individuals for providing various government services and harness the power of JAM (Jan Dhan-Aadhar-Mobile) Trinity.

11.4.2 Panic Button: A Gazette Notification was issued on April 22, 2016 for implementation of panic button feature in all mobile phone handsets. Mobile phone handset manufacturers have intimated that they have implemented panic button in all their mobile handsets (smart as well as feature phones) that are being sold in India from March 1, 2017. GPS facility in mobile phone handsets is mandatory w.e.f. January 1, 2018.

11.4.3 Single number 112: Instructions with regard to single emergency number 112 along with detailed operational guidelines in this regard were issued to all Telecom Service Providers on May 4, 2016. DOT has instructed TSPs to map Single Emergency Number 112 with existing Emergency Number 100 in all state/UTs in August 2016. At present Single Emergency Number 112 is operational with mapped on existing emergency number 100 in all state/UT except Delhi. 112 is designed to be used to replace the multiplicity of Emergency Numbers operations in India such as 100, 101, 102 and 108 etc. The project is to be made operational by all States/UTs under the supervision of Ministry of Home Affairs through PSAP (Public Safety Answering Point). When an emergency call is received at the PSAP, it would be answered by a specially trained officer/call taker/operator of respective state/UT that will transfer the call on the type of emergency, dispatchers to police, fire medical and other response mechanisms.

11.4.4 Aadhaar Based E-KYC for New Subscribers: The Government has prescribed an Aadhaar-based E-KYC services for issuing mobile connections from September 2016.

Under this, a subscriber can authenticate himself using his biometrics at the point of sale and obtain a new activated sim card in 30 minutes. When manually done, this process takes almost a day and involves a lot of paper work. In addition to simplifying the process this also ensures security assurance and is an environment friendly measure saving more than 50,000 trees annually.

11.5 Telecommunications Regulatory Authority of India (TRAI)

TRAI performs the regulatory functions of telecom sector. It has taken various measures in recent years with a view to obtain a sound framework for competition between multiple technologies and vendors.

The quality of services of all service providers is being monitored by TRAI on the basis of quarterly reports submitted by them. TRAI is also conducting an objective survey of quality of service (QoS) parameters of basic and cellular service in different circles through an independent agency. The agency has also been assigned the task of making an assessment of customer satisfaction through a survey. TRAI has also issued a regulation on quality of service for voice over internet protocol (VOIP) based international long distance service.

It has issued guidelines to service providers in respect of pre-paid cards which would enable increased consumer awareness and transparency for the subscriber.

TRAI has played catalytic role in the development of the telecom, broadcasting and cable services. It has been its endeavour to provide an environment, which is fair and transparent, encourages competition, promotes a level-playing field for all service providers, protects the interest of consumers and enables technological benefits to one and all.

TRAI has also taken steps to ensure the quality of service provided by the service providers by way of monitoring the performance of basic and cellular mobile telephone service on quarterly basis and point of interconnection (POI) congestion on monthly basis. The regulatory measures taken by TRAI facilitate orderly growth of telecom sector by promoting healthy competition and enhancing investment efficiency besides protecting the interest of consumers.

11.6 Information Technology (IT) and IT-Enabled Services

India has emerged in recent years as the most preferred destination for outsourcing of IT services. The vibrant IT industry is contributing immensely by providing information about latest technology and international business practices. Various sectors of the Indian economy such as industry, finance, insurance, communications and transport have adopted information technology in a big way. However, agricultural sector of the economy is lagging behind in utilizing IT services. Some efforts have been made in this regard but they are by no means adequate.

IT has been contributing substantially to the economic growth of the country. More importantly, it can immensely help in accelerating the growth momentum by enhancing efficiency, competitiveness and technological edge across sectors, including particularly strategic sectors. Equally significant is the contribution of IT in enabling inclusive growth and development, and in ensuring that people across the length and breadth of the country have access to the opportunities generated by growth.

Differential access to economic opportunities across nations that characterized the past has been fundamentally impacted and altered by IT and telecom. The same phenomenon can be exploited to help equalize access to opportunity within the country, straddling urban and rural, rich and poor. Ubiquitous and reliable connectivity holds the key. IT is thus not just a major part of a better future, but more importantly, is the key instrument in realising it. Imagining a credibly optimistic future and designing IT policy to realize that vision, could therefore be a self-fulfilling prophesy.

Right to Information legislation has led to increased demand for information and transparency which can only be met through effective leveraging of technology.

The information technology sector has made remarkable progress in the last decade. It has transformed the world, enabling innovation and enhancing productivity, connecting people and communities, and improving standards of living and providing opportunities across the globe. While changing the way individuals live, interact, and work, IT has also proven to be a key enabler for enhanced competitiveness and economic and societal modernisation, as well as an important instrument for bridging economic and social divides and reducing poverty.

The pace of technological advance is accelerating and electronics is increasingly becoming a ubiquitous and intrinsic part of people's behaviours and social networks as well as of business practices and government activities and service provision. These transformations will continue to guide human progress by further leveraging IT's positive social, political, and economic impact on government, enterprise, and civil society alike.

11.7 Information Technology Act (ITA), 2000

On January 30, 1997, the United Nations General Assembly adopted, through a Resolution, the Model Law on Electronic Commerce adopted by the United Nations Commission on International Trade Law. This is referred to as the UNCITRAL Model Law on E-Commerce.

Following the UN Resolution, India Parliament passed the Information Technology Act (ITA), 2000 in May 2000 and notified it for effectiveness on October 17, 2000.

ITA, 2000 consisted of 94 sections segregated into 13 chapters. Four schedules also formed part of the Act.

ITA, 2000 addressed the following issues:

1. Legal recognition of electronic documents.
2. Legal recognition of digital signatures.

3. Offences and contraventions.
4. Justice Dispensation System for cyber crimes.

ITA, 2000 was substantially amended through the Information Technology Amendment Act, 2008 which was passed by the two houses of the Indian Parliament on December 23 and 24, 2008. It got the Presidential assent on February 5, 2009 and was notified for effectiveness on October 27, 2009.

In the 2008 version of the Act, there are 124 sections (excluding 5 sections that have been omitted from the earlier version) and 14 chapters. Schedule I and II have been replaced. Schedules III and IV are deleted.

ITA, 2008 as the new version of ITA, 2000 has provided additional focus on Information Security. It has added several new sections on offences including Cyber Terrorism and Data Protection.

The amendment was passed in an eventful Parliamentary session on December 23, 2008 with no discussion in the House. Some of the cyber law observers criticised the amendments on the ground of lack of legal and procedural safeguards to prevent violation of civil liberties of Indians. There has also been appreciation about the amendments from many observers because it addresses the issue of cyber security.

11.8 Ministry of Electronics and Information Technology (MeitY)

MeitY was carved out of Ministry of Communications and Information Technology on July 19, 2016.

11.8.1 Vision: e-Development of India as the engine for transition into a developed nation and an empowered society.

11.8.2 Mission: To promote e-Governance for empowering citizens, promoting the inclusive and sustainable growth of the electronics, IT & ITeS industries, enhancing India's role in internet governance, adopting a multipronged approach that includes development of human resources, promoting R&D and innovation, enhancing efficiency through digital services and ensuring a secure cyber space.

11.8.3 Objectives: These are as under:

1. **e-Government:** Providing e-infrastructure for delivery of e-services.
2. **e-Industry:** Promotion of electronics hardware manufacturing and IT-ITeS industry.
3. **e-Innovation/R&D:** Implementation of R&D Framework: Enabling creation of Innovation/R&D infrastructure in emerging areas of ICT&E/Establishment of mechanism for R&D translation.
4. **e-Learning:** Providing support for development of e-skills and knowledge network.
5. **e-Security:** Securing India's cyber space.
6. **e-Inclusion:** Promoting the use of ICT for more inclusive growth.
7. **Internet Governance:** Enhancing India's role in global platforms of internet governance.

11.8.4 Functions: These are as under:

1. Policy matters relating to information technology, electronics and internet (all matters other than licensing of Internet Service Providers).
2. Promotion of internet, IT and IT-enabled services.
3. Promotion of digital transactions including digital payments.
4. Assistance to other departments in the promotion of e-governance, e-commerce, e- medicine, e-infrastructure etc.
5. Promotion of information technology education and information technology-based education.
6. Matters relating to cyber laws, administration of the Information Technology Act, 2000 and other IT-related laws.
7. Matters relating to promotion and manufacturing of semiconductor devices in the country excluding all matters relating to Semiconductor Complex Limited (SCL), Mohali.
8. Interaction in IT-related matters with international agencies and bodies, e.g. Internet for Business Limited (IFB), Institute for Education in Information Society (IBI) and International

Code Council–online (ICC).

9. Matters relating to Digital India Corporation.
10. Testing and quality in IT and standardization of procedure for IT application and tasks.
11. Electronics Export and Computer Software Promotion Council (ESC).
12. National Informatics Centre (NIC).
13. Initiatives for development of hardware/software industry including knowledge– based enterprises, measures for promoting IT exports and competitiveness of the industry.
14. Unique Identification Authority of India (UIDAI).

11.9 India as Destination for Outsourcing IT and IT-enabled Services

Starting out with basic data entry tasks, IT industry rapidly acquired a reputation as the primary low-cost destination for voice-based customer contact/support services, finance and accounting, and a range of back-office processing activities. The past few years have seen the scope of these services expanding to include increasingly more complex processes involving rule-based decision-making and research/analytics services requiring informed individual judgment and domain/vertical knowledge. Key categories within horizontal IT services include: (a) customer interaction and support (CIS), (b) finance and accounting (F&A) and other related processing services, (c) knowledge services and (d) human resource management (HRM).

With experience and maturity, several providers are also beginning to develop increasing vertical specialization, thereby complementing their horizontal IT service offerings with vertical specific services.

Much of the IT work is of a routine nature such as customer contact services, but increasingly the outsourced jobs are getting sophisticated. The main knowledge services already outsourced to Indian companies are animation and simulation services, data research and analytics, and litigation services.

Other possibilities are in intellectual property research, medical content and services, pharmaceutical services, writing/content development services, database development services and end-to-end logistic invoice services. The big impediment in India making progress from data processing and customer contact services to knowledge process services is deficiency in qualified talent in both quantitative and qualitative terms in economics and statistics, law, medical science, pharmacy, media and English language in particular.

12

Special Economic Zones (SEZs)

12.1 Economics of SEZs

SEZs are geographical regions in a country subject to economic laws which are liberal than typical economic laws of that country. The word *special* mainly means special economic system and policies. A SEZ can be deemed as a *foreign territory* for the purposes of trade operations, duties and tariffs. Units in SEZs enjoy lot of fiscal pampering.

SEZs are self-contained islands providing high-quality infrastructural facilities. SEZs offer industrial, residential and commercial areas with developed plots/pre-built factories, power, telecommunications, water supply, sewerage and drainage, and educational and medical facilities.

SEZs have been established in several countries, including China, India, Iran, Jordan, Poland, Kazakhstan, Philippines and Russia. SEZs are known by different names in different countries. Some close variants of SEZs are growth centres, industrial estates, export zones, industrial parks etc. In the United States, SEZ are referred to as urban enterprise zones.

12.1.1 Types of SEZs: SEZs can be developed either as general SEZs, catering to all types of industries or specialised SEZs, focusing on a specific industry, such as chemicals, automobiles or software. A specialised SEZ offers an opportunity for the industries in the zone to synergise their operations with the local industries in the region, and position themselves close to the local raw material sources. The zone can offer specific facilities such as a common effluent ...atment plant, integrated design centre etc. to cater to the ... of the target industries. However, development of such a ...olves high risk and requires a longer time to sell the ...plots or pre-built factories. Therefore, a specialised

SEZ is viable only in industries like information technology, plasters and textiles which are fast growing and have a large market.

SEZs are of varying sizes in terms of land occupied. A SEZ may be as small in size as 10 hectares. It can be as large as a self-contained township across thousands of hectares having airports, roads, hospitals, schools, movie theatres, shopping malls, homes and manicured parks.

12.1.2 Configuration of a SEZ: Normally a SEZ is divided into three zones.

1. The industrial zone encompasses industrial units catering to both domestic and export markets. It offers two options for entrepreneurs: (a) developed land and (b) pre-built factory space.
2. The residential zone houses the employees of the units. Additionally, in order to commercially exploit certain locational advantages, a portion may be developed for sale to outsiders.
3. The commercial zone provides facilities such as offices, banks, post and telecom services, shopping centres, restaurants, clubs and recreation facilities.

12.1.3 Advantages of SEZs: In the context of the huge demand-supply gap in infrastructure, SEZs are ideal vehicles for providing integrated infrastructural facilities. SEZs are essential for industrialisation in developing countries which, unlike the developed world, do not have uniformly good infrastructural facilities across regions. They can serve as an intermediate solution to the lack of well-developed and uniformly good infrastructural services.

SEZs have been used as engines of growth by many Asian countries such as China, Thailand, Indonesia, Malaysia and Singapore.

Following are the advantages of setting up SEZs:

1. Developed plots and pre-built factories mean that the entrepreneur can immediately set up an industrial unit without spending scarce resources in developing the

necessary infrastructure and land by himself. He also saves on costs because the cost of development is spread over a large number of users.

2. SEZs can serve as catalysts for the development of surrounding region by providing opportunities for employment and creation of ancillary industries.
3. They can help develop social infrastructure like healthcare centres, educational and training facilities. They provide an opportunity to cross-subsidise development and maintenance costs of social infrastructure with surpluses from other components through a common implementing agency.
4. SEZs can be tailored to capitalise on the strengths and needs of a region such as traditional skills and industries, availability of raw materials and locational advantages. Industrial units in the SEZs can take advantage of the synergies arising from forward and backward integration with others in the same sector.
5. SEZs can also act as incubators of small and medium industries until the time these are ready to stand on their own feet.

12.1.4 Pre-conditions for the Success of SEZs: These can be listed as follows:

1. The location of a SEZ is the key factor determining its success. The location should be decided based on an analysis of the competitive advantage and inherent strengths of the region.
2. As foreign direct investment is very important for the success of SEZs, the foreign investment policy with reference to the SEZs should be clarified. Establishment of holding companies for investment in the SEZs should be encouraged.
3. Land acquisition by the private sector should be in tune with the policy of commercialisation of SEZs through private sector participation. In this case, terms of negotiated land purchase should be primarily determined by the market forces. The government may acquire land in

exceptional cases where private sector acquisition of land is difficult and where there is a clear case for public good in the acquisition of the land.

4. Since compensation for the land acquired is often a major cause for dissatisfaction, an independent valuer should be asked to fix the price which should be related to the average of the market prices in the recent past. The government should also encourage the provision of alternative locations for displaced owners. It should be recognised that the government should assist in the land acquisition process and not fix any price.
5. The government should announce a comprehensive legal policy for SEZs based on transparency and enforceability. It is essential to recognise SEZs as infrastructure projects and provide the same incentives including tax/tariff reliefs and special dispensations that are available to an infrastructure project in the power, telecommunications or transport sector.
6. A promotional authority may be set up in each state, on the lines of bodies such as the Industrial Estates Authority of Thailand, as a one-stop agency involved in development of SEZs either by itself or through joint ventures with the private sector. The authority should focus on monitoring and adjudicating.
7. Uninterrupted and quality power supply is a key success factor for any SEZ. State governments should encourage the supply of adequate power to the SEZs either through small captive power plants or through the support of the State Electricity Boards (SEBs) which must announce a clear policy for cogeneration so that captive power plants set up to serve SEZs can be of economic size.
8. Adequate financing through long-term debt is of critical importance for the projects. SEZs should be eligible to receive financing.
9. In order to encourage private sector financing of SEZs, financial institutions providing loans to SEZs may also be

granted exemption from income tax on the profits from loans to SEZs. To encourage further investments in SEZs and also to discourage repatriation by foreign investors, tax rebate may be allowed on profits reinvested in the SEZs or in any other infrastructure project.

10. SEZs must develop connection with technological research institutions, universities, colleges and technical training institutes. Also, appropriate linkages are necessary with transportation facilities such as airports, ports, and railway terminals.

12.1.5 Possible Reasons for the Failure of a SEZ: These can be as follows:

1. Poor location of the SEZ.
2. Improper implementation and design leading to poor quality of infrastructure facilities.
3. Lack of funds.
4. SEZ having been built without tailoring it to the characteristics of that region.
5. Frequent changes in administrative heads and political interference.

12.1.6 Role of the Private Sector: Participation of the private sector in partnership with the government in ownership and operation of SEZs helps in the emergence of a more commercial approach. Private sector participation generally leads to the following favourable effects:

1. Competition resulting in better services and an increase in efficiency in design and focus of the SEZ, its implementation and operation.
2. Greater accountability and responsibility.
3. Professional management.
4. Use of appropriate technologies.
5. Innovation and dynamism in the design and management of the SEZ.
6. Fund mobilisation from private sector to bridge the gap due to lack of government funds.

The commitment of the project sponsors through their

financial and managerial inputs, the immense opportunities for generating profits and surpluses and the competition due to an increase in the number of players would lead to proper choice of the location, design and development of infrastructural facilities.

12.1.7 SEZs and Small Enterprises: Very large industries are capable to acquire large tracts of land and create all necessary infrastructure facilities on their own. Small and medium scale units need quality infrastructure but may not have the means to pay for such facilities. For the SEZs to be viable, the user industries must be able to pay for the cost of the services provided. Only industries with a high value addition may be able to afford such high costs of developing infrastructural facilities.

SEZs should be targeted at small and medium scale industries with a focus on high value-added output. Pre-built factories provide readymade factory space which can cater to the needs of small and medium scale industries, serving as incubators before they grow in size and shift to a larger industrial space.

12.2 Special Economic Zones Act, 2005

India was one of the first in Asia to recognize the effectiveness of the export processing zone (EPZ) model in promoting exports, with Asia's first EPZ set up in Kandla (Gujarat) in 1965. However, the EPZs were not able to emerge as effective instruments for export promotion on account of multiplicity of controls and clearances, absence of world-class infrastructure and an unstable fiscal regime.

Considering the need to enhance foreign investment and promote exports from the country and realising the need that level playing field must be made available to the domestic enterprises and manufacturers to be competitive globally, the Special Economic Zones (SEZs) Policy was announced in April 2000. This policy intended to make SEZs an engine for economic growth supported by quality infrastructure complemented by an attractive fiscal package, both at the

Centre and the State level, with the minimum possible regulations. SEZs in India functioned from November 1, 2000 to February 9, 2006 under the provisions of the Foreign Trade Policy and fiscal incentives were made effective through the provisions of relevant statutes.

To instil confidence in investors and signal the Government's commitment to a stable SEZ policy regime and with a view to impart stability to the SEZ regime thereby generating greater economic activity and employment through the establishment of SEZs, a comprehensive draft SEZ Bill was prepared after extensive discussions with the stakeholders. The Special Economic Zones Act, 2005, was passed by Parliament in May 2005 which received Presidential assent on June 23, 2005. After extensive consultations, the SEZ Act, 2005, supported by SEZ Rules, came into effect on February 10, 2006, providing for drastic simplification of procedures and for single window clearance on matters relating to Central as well as State Governments. The main objectives of the SEZ Act are the following:

1. Generation of additional economic activity.
2. Promotion of exports of goods and services.
3. Promotion of investment from domestic and foreign sources.
4. Creation of employment opportunities.
5. Development of infrastructure facilities.

The SEZ Act, 2005 envisages key role for the State Governments in export promotion and creation of related infrastructure. A single window SEZ approval mechanism has been provided through a 19 member inter-ministerial SEZ Board of Approval (BoA). The applications duly recommended by the respective State Governments/UT Administrations are considered by BoA periodically. All decisions of the BoA are with consensus.

The SEZ Rules provide for differentiated minimum land requirements for different classes of SEZs. Every SEZ is divided into a processing area where alone the SEZ units would come up and the non-processing area where supporting infrastructure is to be created. The SEZ Rules also provide for simplified procedures for development, operation and maintenance of the SEZ, setting up units in SEZs, single window clearance both relating to Central as well as State Governments for setting up of an SEZ and units in a SEZ, and simplified compliance procedures/documentation with emphasis on self-certification. A Board of Approval has been constituted by Government in exercise of the powers conferred under the SEZ Act.

SEZs in India seek to promote value addition component in exports, generate employment and mobilize foreign exchange. SEZs when operational are expected to offer high quality infrastructure facilities and support services, besides allowing for the duty free import of capital goods and raw materials. Additionally, attractive fiscal incentives and simpler customs, banking and other procedures are offered in such zones. Setting up of SEZs is also treated as an infrastructure development activity and offered same incentives. SEZs in India closely follow the Chinese model.

SEZs are intended as engine for economic growth supported by quality infrastructure, with minimum possible regulations, and an attractive fiscal package, both at the level of Central and State Governments.

Various incentives and facilities are offered to both SEZ developers and units in SEZs for attracting investments, including foreign investment, into SEZs. These incentives and facilities are expected to trigger a large flow of foreign and domestic investment in SEZs, in infrastructure and productive capacity, leading to generation of additional economic activity and creation of employment opportunities.

12.3 Approval Mechanism and Administrative Set-up of SEZs

12.3.1 Approval Mechanism: The developer submits the proposal for establishment of SEZ to the concerned State

Government. The State Government has to forward the proposal with its recommendation within 45 days from the date of receipt of such proposal to the BoA. The applicant also has the option to submit the proposal directly to the BoA.

BoA has been constituted by the Central Government in exercise of the powers conferred under the SEZ Act. All the decisions are taken in the BoA by consensus. BoA has 19 Members. It is headed by the Secretary, Department of Commerce in the Ministry of Commerce and Industry, Government of India.

12.3.2 Administrative Set up: The functioning of the SEZs is governed by a three- tier administrative set up. BoA is the apex body and is headed by the Secretary, Department of Commerce. The Approval Committee at the Zone level deals with approval of units in the SEZs and other related issues. Each Zone is headed by a Development Commissioner, who is ex-officio chairperson of the Approval Committee.

Once an SEZ has been approved by the BoA and Central Government has notified the area of the SEZ, units are allowed to be set up in the SEZ. All the proposals for setting up of units in the SEZ are approved at the Zone level by the Approval Committee consisting of Development Commissioner, Customs Authorities and representatives of State Government. All post-approval clearances including grant of importer-exporter code number, change in the name of the company or implementing agency, broad banding diversification etc. are given at the Zone level by the Development Commissioner. The performance of SEZ units is periodically monitored by the Approval Committee and units are liable for penal action under the provision of Foreign Trade (Development and Regulation) Act, 1992 in case of violation of the conditions of the approval.

12.4 Criteria for Approval

Proposals for setting up SEZ in the public/private/joint/State sector are required to meet the following conditions:

1. Minimum size of the SEZ shall not be less than 1,000

hectares. This would however, not apply to existing EPZs converting into SEZs as such or for notifying additional area as a part of such SEZ or to product-specific port/airport based SEZs.

2. SEZ and units therein shall abide by local laws, rules, regulations or by-laws in regard to area planning, sewerage disposal, pollution control and the like. They shall also comply with industrial and labour laws and such other laws/rules and regulations as may be locally applicable.
3. SEZs shall make adequate arrangements to fulfil all the requirements of the laws, rules and procedures applicable to such SEZs.
4. Only units approved under the SEZ scheme would be permitted to be located in SEZ.

Proposals received for setting up of SEZs are considered by an Inter-Ministerial Committee known as the Board of Approval (BOA), in its meeting held every month. The promoters of the SEZs are also invited to such meetings to explain the salient features of their proposals and to furnish clarifications, wherever required.

Proposals that are received up to 15 days prior to the scheduled meeting of the Board of Approval are placed for its consideration and any proposals received thereafter are considered in the next meeting.

12.5 Incentives and Facilities

12.5.1 For Units in SEZ: The incentives and facilities offered to the units in SEZs for attracting investments into the SEZs, including foreign investment, include the following:

1. Duty free import/domestic procurement of goods for development, operation and maintenance of SEZ units.
2. 100 percent income tax exemption on export income for SEZ units under Section 10AA of the Income Tax Act for first 5 years, 50 percent for next 5 years thereafter and 50 percent of the ploughed back export profit for next 5 years.
3. Exemption from minimum alternate tax under Section

115JB of the Income Tax Act.

4. All exports (whether of goods or services) as well as supplies to SEZs have been categorized as zero-rated supplies in the Integrated Goods and Services Tax (IGST) Act, 2017.
5. External commercial borrowing by SEZ units up to US$ 500 million in a year without any maturity restriction through recognized banking channels.
6. Single window clearance for Central and State level approvals.

12.5.2 For Developers of SEZ: These include the following:

1. Exemption from customs/excise duties for development of SEZs for authorized operations approved by the BoA.
2. Income tax exemption on income derived from the business of development of the SEZ in a block of 10 years in 15 years under Section 80-IAB of the Income Tax Act.

12.6 Apprehensions and Concerns

Concerns have been expressed regarding acquisition of agricultural land for setting up SEZs. The State Governments have been advised that in land acquisition for SEZs, first priority should be for acquisition of waste and barren land and if necessary single crop agricultural land could be acquired for the SEZs. If perforce a portion of double cropped agricultural land has to be acquired to meet the minimum area requirements, especially for multi-product SEZ, the same should not exceed 10 percent of the total land required for the SEZ. Various issues relating to setting up of SEZs in the country including issues raised by various political parties are being addressed by the Empowered Group of Ministers.

Some of the apprehensions against the SEZs are the following:

1. Generation of little new activity as there may be relocation of industries to take advantage of tax concessions.
2. Revenue loss.
3. Large-scale land acquisition by the developers which may

lead to displacement of farmers with meagre compensation.

4. Acquisition of prime agricultural land having serious implications for food security.
5. Misuse of land by the developers for real estate.
6. Uneven growth aggravating regional inequalities.

Many of these apprehensions, however, can be addressed through appropriate policies and safeguards.

12.6.1 SEZs and National Security: SEZs coming up in different parts of India have raised security concerns in government circles, particularly the Home Ministry. Government is reluctant to allow any SEZ near the border, fearing threat to national security. All zones with a port or near an existing dock are being closely watched. However, the government-owned Kandla Port Trust, which is setting up a ₹ 7,300 crore port-based zone, has been allowed to proceed further with the project. Similarly, doubts are being raised about gems and jewellery SEZs on the ground that operating units could smuggle precious metals and stones in and out of the country. Furthermore, pharmaceutical industry is also on the watch list. The Home Ministry wants a stricter dispensation for companies undertaking DNA-related work in the SEZs. Government's thinking in clear on the subject, i.e. country's security is paramount and any unit in a SEZ could be shut down the moment it is found to be indulging in anything that is detrimental to national interest.

To sum up, Initiative of the Government of India to set up SEZs on the pattern of China is a welcome change in the strategy for economic development and export promotion. The move is a bold departure and a paradigm shift in the basic approach to development efforts. It is an acknowledgement of the potential of export-led development strategy.

The challenge ahead lies in appropriately sequencing to sustain the popular support for reforms and reconciling the conflicting interests of the various reforms constituencies. The recent debate about SEZ indicates the kind of considerations that have to be taken into account in the formulation of policies. While the initiative on SEZs is laudable, its success will depend on how well the model is evolved and the implementation strategy worked out.

The task ahead is to examine how far the key policy parameters that contributed to the success of SEZs in China have been incorporated in the Indian policy framework. The distinguishing features of Chinese SEZs are their large size, investment friendly customs regime, flexible labour laws, liberal policy for DTA access, attractive package of incentives and delegation of powers in favour of provinces and local authorities for managing the zones.

The process of decentralisation needs to be taken to its logical conclusion by empowering local authorities and State Governments to approve investment proposals. The Central and State Governments should market SEZs aggressively to attract foreign investment. Relaxation of labour laws and rationalisation of duty on DTA access can give a big boost to the scheme.

13

Urban Infrastructure and Services

Rising urbanization in India has increased the functional responsibilities of municipalities. To meet the scale and challenge of urbanization, municipal governments are always looking for additional funds from various sources.

India is a part of the global trend towards increasing urbanization. Cities hold tremendous potential as engines of economic and social development, creating jobs and generating wealth through economies of scale. They need to be sustained and augmented through the high urban productivity for country's economic growth. National economic growth and poverty reduction efforts will be increasingly determined by the productivity of these cities and towns. For Indian cities to become growth oriented and productive, it is essential to achieve a world class urban system. This in turn depends on attaining efficiency and equity in the delivery and financing of urban infrastructure.

13.1 Rising Urbanization in India and its Consequences

Urbanization is directly associated with economic development. In fact, a shift of population from rural to urban areas is an indicator of economic development. The shift of population to urban areas was slow during British rule because the process of economic development itself was slow during that period. Urban population which formed 10 percent of total population in 1911, moderately increased to 14 percent in 1941. This was in sharp contrast to the urbanization trend taking place in Europe.

India ranks poorly among the countries of the world in respect of degree of urbanization. The share of urban population in total population was 25.7 percent in 1991 which increased to 27.8 percent in 2001, as per Census 2001.

About 377 million Indians comprising of about 31 percent of the country's population, live in urban areas according to Census 2011. This is a smaller proportion compared to other large developing countries, for example, 45 percent in China, 54 percent in Indonesia, 78 percent in Mexico and 87 percent in Brazil. With the more rapid growth of the Indian economy in recent years, which is expected to continue, the rate of urbanization will increase. Projections are that by 2031, about 600 million Indians will reside in urban areas.

Rising urbanization in India has led to tremendous pressure on civic infrastructure systems, water supply, sewerage and drainage, uncollected solid waste, parks and open spaces, transport etc. It has also led to deterioration in the quality of city environments. In several cities, the problems of traffic congestion, pollution, poverty, inadequate housing, crime, and social unrest are assuming alarming proportions. Further, growing urbanization is characterized by incomplete devolution of functions to the elected bodies, lack of financial resources, unwillingness to progress towards municipal autonomy, adherence to outdated methods in property taxation, hesitation in levy of user charges, unsatisfactory role of parastatals in the provision of water supply and sanitation services etc.

As the proportion of the urban population continues to grow, investments in urban infrastructure for the provision of services such as roads, water supply and sewerage, transportation and the like will need to be much higher than they have been in the past.

The likely increase in urban productivity and population due to the new economic policies of the Government of India will place a heavy demand on all kinds of urban infrastructure and services. The infrastructure bottlenecks in urban centres are likely to pose serious impediments in enhancing the productivity.

Since a significant part of national income originates in urban areas, efforts must be made to maintain and enhance urban productivity which, in turn, depends on the level and quality of urban infrastructure. The demand for urban infrastructure services has increased, and is likely to accelerate further, due to rising personal incomes, rapid growth of population, and general increase in economic activities. Inability of municipal governments to meet the rising demand would adversely affect growth prospects of the economy.

Urbanization will be central to India's strategy of achieving faster and more inclusive growth because agglomeration and densification of economic activities (and habitations) in urban conglomerations stimulates economic efficiencies and provides more opportunities for earning livelihoods. Thus, urbanization increases avenues for entrepreneurship and employment compared to what is possible in dispersed rural areas. It, thereby, enables faster inclusion of more people in the process of economic growth.

13.2 Features of Urban Infrastructure Services

Urban infrastructure services have the following characteristics:

1. Most urban infrastructure services are natural monopolies and their marginal cost declines over a very large range of output. As such, it is feared that the private sector might exploit the monopolistic situation. Such services include water, waste water management, telephone, electricity, bridge, and road networks.
2. Many services like sanitation and solid waste disposal (SWD) have significant external economies. As a consequence, market-based systems may fail to provide the service in adequate quantity and quality.
3. It is difficult to exclude anyone from using certain public services like roads or street lighting. The consumer may refuse to pay for the service since he may be able to use it free of charge legally or otherwise.
4. Certain infrastructure services being necessities (like water) have almost inelastic demand. Private provision of

these could result in exploitative pricing unless prices are regulated.

5. Requirement of heavy investment in capital equipment discourages private sector entry into certain infrastructure segments.

The above mentioned characteristics have for long been used as valid arguments for blocking entry of the private sector into infrastructure. The arguments, however, are slowly losing their validity due to many technological and organizational innovations. Unbundling of services has been a major mechanism through which the misconception about the economies of scale argument has been overcome. Technological innovations in the areas of sanitation and sewerage have permitted low-cost supply options. Increasing range and quality of service has reduced the cost of providing the service, making the operation commercially viable and also opening up areas for private sector operations. The recognition of the demand aspect has made remunerative pricing possible in some segments.

By and large, governments have not been very effective suppliers of many services. The cost of government failures has been much higher than the possible cost of market failure. Commercialisation of infrastructure projects basically means efficient provision of service to the consumers' satisfaction on cost-recovery basis. Since the public sector in most cases is an inefficient provider due to its inherent characteristics, promotion of privatisation itself becomes an instrument for commercialisation.

13.3 Privatisation of Municipal Services

Municipalities alone cannot handle huge infrastructural projects like water supply, sewage disposal, and urban transport. Involvement of central, state, and private sector is required to meet the scale of investment needed in these areas. Similarly, greater participation of private sector is desirable in the provision of civic services, particularly those the consumption of which can be attributed to individuals and households. There are many types of arrangement in respect of public-private-partnership depending on situation. However, care should be taken not to dilute current social commitments while embarking on public-private-partnership.

The historical and ideological resistance to private sector participation persists in most places. Consequently, few local bodies have tried out private sector participation in civic services on any significant scale. Wherever it has happened, the experiment has remained limited to disposal of solid wastes, and maintenance of parks.

The disenchantment with utility enterprises of municipalities is not conceptual but borne out of their inefficient and sometimes corrupt management. The merits of privatisation are seen in terms of improvement in efficiency and reduction in the budgetary burden of state-owned enterprises.

Though the need for private sector participation is widely felt, it is not openly expressed. Very rarely political parties have spoken publicly against the public sector. Contrarily, there is a stiff opposition by political parties to any move to undermine the importance of public sector. The strong unions of public sector enterprises come in handy for politicians to prevent the erosion of state and municipal activities.

13.4 Urban Housing

Housing is an activity that is typically labour intensive and, therefore, fits in well with the pattern of development envisaged for India. The provision of shelter is a basic need which must be met. Housing construction also creates much-needed employment for the unskilled and, therefore, income for the relatively poor.

The housing problem has become acute in most industrial regions of the world since Second World War. There is increasing recognition everywhere of the close relation between housing and the health and well-being of the people. Actually, over a number of years, shortages on a large-scale have developed and conditions worsened a great deal. Private enterprise has proved incapable of meeting the needs and the State has to assume direct initiative and responsibility in this field to an increasing extent. In some highly industrialised countries, housing accommodation has been provided to a large extent by heavy subsidies from the State in respect of houses of standard design for low-income groups which are not an economic proposition in most countries at present on account of the high cost of construction, building materials and development.

13.4.1 Importance of Housing: In fulfilling the basic needs of the population, housing ranks next only to food and clothing in importance. A certain minimum standard of housing is essential for healthy and civilised existence. The development of housing, therefore, must enjoy high priority in a poor country like India where housing amenities are far below the minimum standards that have been internationally accepted. Housing activity serves to fulfil many of the fundamental objectives of national policies:

1. Providing shelter.
2. Raising the quality of life, particularly of the poorer sections of the population.
3. Creating conditions which are conducive to the achievements of crucial objectives in terms of health, sanitation and education.
4. Creating substantial additional employment and dispersed economic activity.
5. Improving urban-rural and inter-personal equity through the narrowing down of difference in standards of living.
6. Generating additional voluntary savings.

13.4.2 Private Sector Participation: As in the past, the bulk of housing for the higher income groups should continue to be provided by the private sector. In addition, in view of the constraints on public resources, there should be greater encouragement of the private sector to step up its activities in the construction of housing for low and middle income groups. Imaginative schemes of improved facilities for financial intermediation in this sector will have to be investigated in order to achieve this objective.

The public sector has only a marginal, though promotional, role to play in the provision of urban housing. It is clear that the need is great for better and more housing in urban areas. Given the overall resources constraints and more pressing competing claims on public resources, the vast majority of additional housing in urban areas will have to be met from private resources. The role of the public sector will have to be restricted to the improvement of slums, the direct provision of housing to some of the urban poor and encouragement of agencies such as HUDCO which can promote the marshalling of private resource into housing in a constructive manner.

Much of the ills of urban housing and resource mobilisation in larger urban areas can be attributed to the problems inherent in the urban land market. While urban development programmes have to depend largely on a well coordinated land development programme, the existing legal and administrative machinery has impeded supply and development of serviced land. Also, very little efforts have been made to mop up the large appreciation in values of real estate particularly in metropolitan cities.

A corollary to the above process is exploration of avenues through which private initiatives can find a greater role in urban development programme. The role of private sector needs to be expanded. The extent and the manner in which private developers can contribute to urban renewal and squatter settlements and peripheral areas in metropolitan regions (including residential and trunk infrastructure development) needs assessment.

For years to come the bulk of the building activity will still have to be undertaken by private enterprise. In building works on a small scale, the private builder can often construct at a rate cheaper than public bodies on account of economy in supervision and personal attention to details.

At the same time while private builders should be encouraged to the maximum, steps should be taken to eliminate the speculative element in land and to discourage land hoarding in urban areas, for which purpose the taxation structure on vacant lands should be so designed as to make all land hoarding unprofitable.

13.5 Slum Clearance/Development

Most of the towns in India have grown up haphazardly. They have a large proportion of sub-standard houses and slums containing unsanitary mud-huts of flimsy construction, poorly ventilated, over-congested and often lacking in essential amenities such as water and light. This is particularly so in the large industrial cities. The disgraceful sights presented by the slums of Delhi, Mumbai, Kolkata, Chennai and other big cities are conspicuous examples of this state of affairs. These conditions have developed because of insufficient control over building activity by the State or municipal authorities. Local authorities have been generally indifferent to enforcing such by-laws regarding building and sanitation as have existed. Their own resources have been too meagre to permit any development work worth the name.

The migration of people from villages to towns in search of employment has accelerated the growth of urban population. Adequate facilities and services for the increased urban population are not available. There has been some decline in standards, particularly of housing. The provision of housing through private or co-operative effort is usually directed to the affluent or middle classes and the incoming poor in metropolitan areas give rise to slums.

The experience of public housing so far is that its unit costs are high and that with the constraint of resources it is not possible for public operations to touch even the fringe of the problem. Slum clearance schemes often lead to creation of new slums or deterioration of conditions in some of the older slums. In growing cities of a reasonable size, it should be part of Government policy to encourage, through proper planning and land policy, adequate supply of housing. In cities where the slum population is large, this approach would not be effective and it would be necessary to try to ameliorate the living conditions of dwellers of slums as an immediate measure. Emphasis should be on limiting the rise in the prices of land, providing financial assistance to co-operative and private effort and assuming legal powers for reconditioning of slums.

Some of the difficulties which come in the way of implementation of the slum clearance and improvement programme are: (a) lengthy and time-consuming procedures of acquisition of slum areas, (b) non-availability and high costs of alternative sites near existing places of work, (c) inability of the slum dwellers to pay even the subsidised rent and (d) their reluctance to move from the areas selected for clearance.

The strategy of attempting massive relocation of slums in urban areas has also found critics. Such relocation not only involves substantial hardship to those affected in terms of loss of easy access to employment centres and other amenities, but results in unnecessary destruction of existing housing capital, however sub-standard it may be. It is, therefore, important that substantially increased investments be made in the environmental improvement of slum areas. Low cost sanitation and drainage are key areas of much needed investment in the slums of our cities.

While steps should be taken to clear/improve existing slums, it is equally important that new slums are not allowed to grow up. This is by no means an easy task to accomplish. Besides preparing and strictly implementing master plans for all growing towns and cities, it is essential to enforce municipal by-laws and building regulations, and at the same time, to expand housing facilities for low-income groups and for economically weaker sections. As transitional measures, night shelters and dormitory accommodation for pavement dwellers and non-family workers have considerable urgency. Similarly, the housing of sweepers and scavengers must receive special attention. In selecting slum areas for clearance and improvement high priority should be given to areas predominantly inhabited by sweepers and scavengers.

Housing provides a large scope for direct and indirect employment of persons with a wide range of skills and also of unskilled persons. Housing is a basic necessity as well as an important economic activity, in that it is a part of the construction industry. It is clear that housing conditions in the country are rather poor. A large number of people either live without any shelter whatsoever or in units below the lowest possible standards.

With the anticipated entry of FDI into the real estate sector, care has to be taken that the needs of the urban poor and marginalised sections are not ignored. Given the large number of activities impinging on housing directly and indirectly and the multiplicity of agencies involved, designing a framework for orderly and dynamic growth in the housing sector is a challenge to the planners.

13.6 Urban Transport

13.6.1 Need for Efficient Urban Transport: Urban transport is one of the key elements of urban infrastructure. An effective urban transportation system enhances productivity and growth in the economy. Urban transportation covers two broad modes, viz. private transport and public transport. Public transport is energy-efficient and less polluting. Public transport system also helps to maximize urban-rural linkage and improves access of the rural/semi-urban population in the periphery to the city centres for the movement of labour without proliferation of slums within and around cities.

A good network of roads coupled with efficient mass urban transport system makes a substantial contribution to the efficiency of the cities and enables them to become a catalyst of economic and social development.

Little attention has been paid to development of mass rapid transport systems in most major cities. In fact, urban transport is one of the most important components of urban infrastructure which has been neglected due to various reasons. Bus services and urban rail services have been extremely limited.

Till recently, the city of Delhi lacked an efficient mass transport system. The setting up of the Delhi Metro Rail Transit System (DMRTS), which was inaugurated on December 24, 2002, has brought about a great improvement in efficiency and quality of life of the citizens of Delhi. DMRTS is a joint venture between Government of India and Delhi Government. DMRTS is one of the largest infrastructure projects being undertaken, and is being developed on lines of mass rapid transit systems in Hong Kong and Singapore. The project is expected to bring about substantial reduction in pollution, reduction in accident rates and improvement in quality of life.

The objective of urban transport policy should be to ensure safe, affordable, quick, comfortable, reliable and sustainable access for the growing number of city residents to jobs, education, recreation and such other needs within our cities.

13.6.2 Transport Problems in Urban Areas: For urban areas to be able to support the required level of economic activity, they must provide for the easy and sustainable flow of goods and people. Unfortunately, however, such flow of goods and people has been facing several problems. Most prominent among them are the following:

1. Accessing jobs, education, recreation and similar activities is becoming increasingly time-consuming. Billions of man hours are lost with people stuck in traffic. The primary reason for this has been the explosive growth in the number of motor vehicles, coupled with limitations on the amount of road space that can be provided.
2. Cost of travel, especially for the poor, has increased considerably. This is largely because the use of cheaper non-motorised modes like cycling and walking has become extremely risky, since these modes have to share the same right of way with motorized modes. Further, with population growth, cities have tended to sprawl and increased travel distances have made non-motorized modes impossible to use. This has made access to

livelihoods, particularly for the poor, far more difficult.

3. Travel in the city has become more risky with accident rates having gone up. The number of persons killed in road accidents has also gone up. This again has tended to impact the poor more severely as many of those killed or injured tend to be cyclists, pedestrians or pavement dwellers.
4. Increased use of personal vehicles has led to increased air pollution.

Unless the above problems are remedied, poor mobility can become a major dampener to economic growth and cause the quality of life to deteriorate. A policy is, therefore, needed on the approach to dealing with this rapidly growing problem as also offer a clear direction and a framework for future action.

13.6.3 Private Sector Participation: It is evident that huge capital investments are required in dealing with the urban transport problems. Whether they are for constructing capital-intensive mass transit systems or segregated rights-of-way for cycles and pedestrians, a substantial financial burden would devolve on the government. Most State Governments and local bodies do not have the required resources and, therefore, alternative methods of financing would have to be explored.

The Central and State Governments should encourage partnerships and greater use of private capital in areas where the private sector can competitively deliver urban transport services. More specifically, the greater use of private buses in city areas should be encouraged to reduce the dependence on public budgets. The commercial utilization of land resources, available with public transport service providers should be encouraged to raise additional resources.

There are several activities in which the private sector can be beneficially engaged, thereby saving financial resources for activities that only public agencies can best perform. However, these have to be done under conditions that strike a fair balance between the universal obligations of the government and the profit motive of the private operator. Accordingly,

Central and State Governments should encourage a more liberal use of the private sector, especially in activities like the operation and maintenance of parking facilities certification facilities, repair facilities, construction and management of terminal facilities etc.

Till the mid-1980s most public transport services were largely provided by publicly-owned State Transport Corporations. Since then, however, some States have permitted privately-run services. While public operations have tended to be high cost and most State Transport Corporations have run up heavy losses, the reliability and safety record of inadequately regulated private operators has been poor. Thus, State Governments should involve the private sector in providing public transport services, but under well-structured procurement contracts.

13.7 Urban Water Supply

Ministry of Urban Development, Government of India is responsible for formulation of broad policies and programmes and assists State Governments/UTs in providing technical assistance in water supply and sanitation sector.

13.7.1 Public-Private-Partnerships (PPPs): PPPs have been explored in India's urban water supply services since the 1990s. Several projects have been attempted with varying roles and extent of participation envisaged for the private sector. These attempts have had mixed outcomes: while several projects planned during the initial years were abandoned in the development phase, there has been an increase in the number of contracts awarded to the private sector in recent years. Further, the nature and type of projects developed on a PPP basis have also changed. There is now an increased recognition of the fact that PPPs in urban water supply services have evolved significantly since the earlier years.

14

Healthcare Services

Human resources are a country's most precious endowment. The success of a development strategy depends on the extent to which human resources are developed in terms of education, skills, health and well-being. The programmes initiated and executed since Independence have strengthened the healthcare system in the country and yielded considerable dividends, particularly in the field of communicable diseases. Measures have been initiated to correct the regional imbalances prevalent within the system, to improve referral services and to augment health-care services in the rural areas.

14.1 Importance of Health

Human resources are a country's most precious endowment. The success of a development strategy depends on the extent to which human resources are developed in terms of education, skills, health and well-being. The programmes initiated and executed since Independence have strengthened the healthcare system in the country and yielded considerable dividends, particularly in the field of communicable diseases. Measures have been initiated to correct the regional imbalances prevalent within the system, to improve referral services and to augment health-care services in the rural areas.

Good health is both an end in itself and also contributes to economic growth. Meeting the health needs of the population requires a comprehensive and sustained approach. Health services should be affordable and of reasonable quality.

Health is fundamental to national progress in any sphere. In terms of resources for economic development, nothing can be considered of higher importance than the health of the people which is a measure of their energy and capacity as well as of the potential of man-hours for productive work in relation to the total number of persons maintained by the nation. For the efficiency of industry and of agriculture, the health of the worker is an essential consideration.

Health is a positive state of well being in which the harmonious development of physical and mental capacities of the individual lead to the enjoyment of a rich and full life. It is not a negative state of mere absence of disease. Health further implies complete adjustment of the individual to his total environment, physical and social. Health involves primarily the application of medical science for the benefit of the individual and of society. However, many other factors, social, economic and educational have an intimate bearing on the .health of the community. Health is thus a vital part of a concurrent and integrated programme of development of all aspects of community life.

The output of the industrial worker in India is low compared with that of the worker in other countries. The productive capacity of the agricultural worker is comparatively low. The loss caused by morbidity in working time is enormous. To this must be added the expenditure to the individual and to the State in the provision of medical care.

There is a strong link between poverty and ill-health. Ill health creates immense stress even among those who are financially secure. Onset of a long and expensive illness can drive the economically well-off into poverty. The importance of public provisioning of quality healthcare to enable access to affordable and reliable heath services cannot be underestimated. This is specially so in the context of preventing the non-poor from entering into poverty and reducing the suffering of those who are already below poverty line.

An investment in health is investment in man and on improving the quality of his life. It is, therefore, well-recognised that health has to be viewed in its totality, as a part of the strategy of human resources development. Horizontal and vertical linkages have to be established among all the interrelated programmes like protected water supply, environmental sanitation and hygiene, nutrition, education, family planning and maternity and child welfare. Only with such linkages can the benefits of various programmes be optimised. An attack on the problem of diseases cannot be entirely successful unless it is accompanied by an attack on poverty itself which is the main cause of it.

14.2 Current Health Services Scenario in India

Improvement in the health status of the population is a major thrust area under the social development programmes being undertaken in the country. This is sought to the achieved through improvement in the access to and utilization of health services in the country with special focus on under-served and under-privileged segments of the population. India has built up a vast health infrastructure and manpower at primary, secondary and tertiary care in government, voluntary and private sectors.

Technological advances and improvement in access to healthcare technologies have resulted in a substantial improvement in health indices of the population and a steep decline in mortality. However, the extent of access to and utilization of healthcare has varied substantially between States, districts and different segments of society.

Urban growth has led to increase in number of urban poor. Though the coverage of health and family welfare services in urban areas is much better than the rural, lack of water and sanitation and the high population density in slums leads to rapid spread of infections. These settlements have high incidence of vector borne diseases, asthma, TB, malaria, coronary heart diseases, diabetes etc. Poor housing conditions, exposure to heat and cold, air and water pollution and occupational hazards add to the environmental risks for the poor. They are further made vulnerable, as they have no back up savings, food stocks or social support systems to tide over the crisis of illness. Despite the presence of so many private and government hospitals in urban areas, large chunk of homeless and those living in slums or temporary settlements are left out of the proper healthcare system. Thus, even though there is a concentration of healthcare facilities in urban areas, the urban poor lack access to them and initiatives in this regard have been limited and fragmented.

From the healthcare access point of view, public health services infrastructure is well-developed in India, starting from primary care facilities [such as the sub-centres, primary health centres (PHCs) and community health centres (CHCs)], and secondary care facilities (such as the sub-district and district hospitals), and tertiary care facilities (such as medical colleges and specialty hospitals).

Efforts are continuing to improve the access to and utilization of health, family welfare and nutrition services with special focus on under-served and under-privileged segments of population. Technological improvements and increased access to healthcare have resulted in a steep fall in mortality rate, but the burden of communicable and non-communicable diseases, environmental pollution and nutritional problems continues to be high. In spite of the fact that norms for creation of infrastructure and manpower are similar throughout the country, there remain substantial variations among states and districts within a state in availability and utilization of healthcare services and health indices of the population.

Current policies and programmes are aimed to provide essential supplies, improve efficiency and ensure accountability especially in states where performance is sub-optimal. In view of the massive inter-regional differences in the availability and utilization of health services and health indices of the population, a differential strategy is envisaged so that there is incremental improvement in all states and districts within a state. This in turn is expected to result in substantial improvement in state and national indices and enable the country to achieve the goals set for the future.

A transition from high incidence of morbidity and

mortality to a state where people generally enjoy long and disease free life is a desirable and valued social change. There will have to be a continued commitment to provide essential primary healthcare and emergency life-saving services free of cost to individuals based on their needs and not on their ability to pay. At the same time, suitable strategies will have to be evolved, tested and implemented for levying and collecting charges, and utilizing the funds obtained for healthcare services, from people above poverty line.

Presently, India has a vast network of governmental, voluntary and private health infrastructure manned by large number of medical and paramedical persons.

14.3 Growth of Private Sector in Healthcare

The healthcare system in India consists of a public sector and a private sector, which includes informal networks of healthcare providers. The private health sector is large and heterogeneous, and includes for-profit providers of varying capacities, informal providers and NGO providers. India has the largest private health sector in the world in terms of human resources, with over one million qualified doctors of various systems of medicine and approximately 1.25 million unqualified rural medical practitioners.

Further, in both rural and urban areas, a large number of unqualified practitioners also form part of the private sector. The health sector operates in a largely unregulated environment, with minimal supervision over what services can be provided, by whom, in what manner and at what cost. Hence, there are many discrepancies and disparities that occur across the cost, access and quality aspects of Indian health services.

A significant proportion of household expenditure ends up in the unorganised private sector. The formal for-profit sector covers a broad range of facilities from small clinics and nursing homes to large corporate chains of tertiary facilities. Although inequitable, expensive, over-indulgent in clinical procedures and without quality standards or public disclosure of practices, the private sector is perceived to be easily accessible, better managed and more efficient than its public counterpart.

Surveys of health-seeking behaviour in India indicate that the poor increasingly prefer, and use, private providers of healthcare rather than public providers. Private providers are also a major source of care in rural areas with strong networks of private medical practitioners present. Private practitioners are typically the first point of contact that the rural poor have with the health system, largely due to their extensive reach and coverage of the population.

Growth of private health sector in India has been considerable in both provision and financing. There is diversity in the composition of the private sector, which ranges from voluntary, not-for-profit, corporates, trusts, stand-alone specialist services, diagnostic services, pharmacy shops and a range of highly qualified to unqualified providers, each addressing different market segments.

Private sector is flourishing primarily because of the failure of the public sector. The growth of private hospitals and diagnostic centres was also encouraged by the Central and State Governments by offering tax exemptions and land at concessional rates, in return for provision of free treatment for the poor as a certain proportion of outpatients and inpatients. Apart from subsidies, private corporate hospitals receive huge amounts of public funds in the form of reimbursements from the public sector undertakings, the Central and the State governments for treating their employees.

The cost of healthcare in the private sector is much higher than the public sector. Many small providers have poor knowledge base and tend to follow irrational, ineffective and sometimes even harmful practices for treating minor ailments. Bulk of the qualified medical practitioners and nurses are subject to self-regulation by their respective State Medical Councils under central legislation. In practice, however, regulation of these professionals is weak and close to non-existent.

14.4 Public versus Private Hospitals

Unlike private for-profit companies, public organisations are typically faced with the need to achieve complex and sometimes conflicting social outcomes, some of which change relative to each other over time due to the movement of social and economic factors outside of their control. The implicit contract between public actors and society at large is therefore constantly in motion.

For instance, a public hospital has an obligation to respond to all the medical demands and needs of a community. People must be treated regardless of their ability to pay and citizenship. Consideration must therefore be given to medical conditions that pose a risk to the presenting patient and those that pose a wider threat to the community (e.g. infectious diseases). The strategic service mix must therefore be constantly re-evaluated to decide between preventive rather than purely curative approaches.

A private for-profit hospital, by way of contrast, focuses principally on profit maximisation and may be happy to prioritise responses for acute patients where this optimises revenues relative to fixed costs. The health of a community is not their responsibility. A private for-profit facility would not need to internalise complex social concerns unless compelled to do so by government legislation. A profit-oriented hospital can therefore be regarded as efficient in the pursuit of a narrow range of fixed goals, but inefficient in addressing the wider social concerns that typically fall into the remit of a public hospital.

14.5 Public-Private-Partnership (PPP) in Healthcare

The thought of public-private-partnerships (PPPs) for some conjures up the spectre of a private invasion of spaces that should appropriately remain the sole jurisdiction of public authorities of one form or another. Within the sphere of healthcare, access to which is universally regarded as a human right, private motivations for coverage or provision are treated with caution—often rightfully so. For instance, a strong technical consensus exists that unregulated private health markets suffer from various forms of market failure that are ultimately harmful to the general welfare.

Industrialised countries consequently regulate their private markets to ensure access and address market failures. Despite these concerns, there is growing recognition that private markets offer opportunities for public authorities to improve service offerings. Private actors, whether for profit or not-for-profit, are advantaged by an ability to make operational decisions at their discretion, unlike many public sector organisations. While this discretion may be exercised in favour of pure private goals when operating exclusively in the private sector, public actors are able to leverage off this discretion, and its resulting efficiencies, by contractually capturing the purely private goal and directing it towards broader social protection.

PPPs involve a wide spectrum of potential interventions—from strategic financing through to one-off projects. The achievement of public goals through the use of private markets and actors requires that government platforms completely understand how contractual and regulatory frameworks are developed and managed. Once internalised, state actors will be in a strong position to expand the range of development policy instruments at their disposal.

There are many ways to systematically improve the performance of a sector in all countries. These include, inter alia, re-shaping a systems architecture, improving governance through properly designed laws, transparency requirements, independent oversight and compliance regimes, and improved financing and resource allocation.

Many systems are inefficiently structured, with certain functions over-centralised. Correcting the mix of centralised and decentralised functions is therefore an important driver of improved service delivery. Accountability failures are one of the most important areas driving inefficiencies and corruption in health systems. Improved performance is therefore predicated on governance reform.

14.6 Case for PPP in Health Sector

PPP in health sector would make sense when the efficiencies of a private actor's narrow goals could be incorporated into the complex goals of a public organisation. The general case for partnerships could therefore arise for the following reasons:

1. Certain narrow specialised tasks could usefully be contractually allocated to a private party, the performance of which is normally disrupted in the public organisation due to their complex and changing priorities. The contractual nature of the relationship therefore serves to insulate the activity from the kind of unavoidable disruption faced by public organisations.
2. Scale advantages could be achieved where, for instance, a large high-technology business, with a large platform supporting multiple private companies, is able to offer better value at lower cost than would be possible for a public (or private) organisation attempting to in-source the function.
3. Economies of scope are possible where the different capabilities in partner organisations can be accessed and used across the partnership. For instance, specialised accounting, legal, marketing and clinical skills may be present in the one partner but not the other.
4. Mutual learning opportunities can be accessed where more advanced partners can accelerate a catch-up in business practices and the use of technology.
5. Efficiency gains through time can be captured from the competitive bidding process used to allocate and re-allocate a contract.

Aside from the first rationale, all the rest would also apply to the decisions private organisations ordinarily make to engage in partnerships and are therefore not especially tied to the publicness of an enterprise. In some senses, therefore, PPPs could be regarded as a normal opportunity for any organisation, public or private, to improve performance. The only special consideration for public organisations is the complexity of their goals and the fact that they cannot typically access some of the advantages of a partnership by way of acquisition. .They are therefore limited to in-sourcing, contracting-out and PPPs, with the appropriate option based on a case-by-case assessment.

Since the financing, provision and access gaps are great, governments at all levels try to bridge these, at least for the poor, through the promotion of PPPs and subsidies of various forms. Public-private partnerships are therefore used as a mechanism to leverage the potential of the private sector to achieve systemic results. Public-private-partnerships are presently viewed as social experiments that offer a mechanism to supplement public health services by engaging and leveraging private actors. It is also believed that certain structural drawbacks of private healthcare delivery can be mitigated to an extent by PPPs. Importantly, private actors are directed through the partnerships toward public objectives–an important objective of PPPs.

14.7 PPP in the Indian Health Sector

The private sector plays an important role in providing various forms of health services in India, although mostly by default. Collaborating with the private sector and fostering partnerships for providing health services to the under-served sections of the population has therefore increased as a policy priority. Due to the deficiencies in the public sector health systems, the poor in India are forced to seek services from the private sector, often borrowing to pay for them out of pocket.

Given the significant presence of the private health sector in the country, especially in secondary, tertiary and support services such as pharmacies and diagnostics, public health systems have little option but to improve access in cooperation with the private sector. Engaging with the private sector therefore offers the opportunity to, inter alia, strengthen public healthcare delivery systems.

The Ministry of Health and Family Welfare (MoHFW), Government of India, has also evolved guidelines for PPPs in different national health programmes such as RNTBCP, NBCP, National Leprosy Eradication Programme and RCH.

The National Rural Health Mission also proposed to support the development and effective implementation of regulatory mechanisms for the private health sector to ensure equity, transparency and accountability in achieving the public health goals.

14.7.1 Partnerships in Health Financing through Health Insurance: The government covers, wholly or partially, the health insurance premium for families below the poverty line (BPL). These families, in turn, are insured against expenses related to health events and hospitalisation, up to a certain amount. The private sector provides the insurance for a range of health services pre-determined by the government while services are delivered at public or private health facilities.

14.7.2 Contracting-in and Contracting-out of Service Delivery: The second major form of partnership in health sector involves contracting for defined services from private providers. In this model, the public sector provides the funds but allows the private partner operational control with monitoring performed by the public sector. The most popular model of contracting is the Chiranjeevi Yojana where the public sector hospital invites private doctors to undertake normal and caesarean deliveries to increase patient volumes at an institution. The contracting model found in almost all parts of India involves the management of primary care by NGOs. Government provides most of the funds to the NGO and they run primary care services for a stipulated period under contract.

14.7.3 Outsourcing of Operations and Management of Public Health Facilities: This involves the management of a part or all of a public facility by the private sector. The private player is paid a fixed fee by the awarding authority for performing specific tasks, the value of which is dependent on the costs and/or risks involved. Such contracts allow the entry of private-sector skills into operations, design, delivery, labour and equipment procurement. Examples include non-clinical hospital services such as laundry, catering, security; the contracting-out of kitchen, cleaning and laundry services; clinical services such as radiology and laboratory services, the directly-observed therapy programme for anti-tubercular therapy; and the private management of primary healthcare centres.

14.7.4 Build-Operate-Transfer (BOT) Model: Here, the private sector is assigned the task of building, operating and eventually transferring the project to the public sector. The model involves outsourcing the early stages of a hospital project's execution. Once the project starts running smoothly, it is taken over and run by the government or a corporate entity. The hospital group will invest in the hospital and operate it for a number of years (usually less than 15 years) before handing it back to the public sector. The hospital group generates financial returns during the years it operates the hospital. Further, the public sector retains the asset and gets a fully-functional hospital at the end of the PPP term.

14.7.5 Concession Model: This works more like a long-term lease where a private player takes over the management of a state-owned enterprise including significant investment risks. The ownership and investment decisions during the lease period therefore no longer remain with the state government.

14.7.6 Joint Venture Model: The project is jointly owned and operated by the public and private sector entities that share costs, risks and revenues. Most of the time, a joint venture is undertaken when the public sector seeks technical skills from a private entity.

14.7.7 Social Franchisee Model: Here one agency—non-government or quasi-government—decides to start a chain of providers. This can be done by converting an existing healthcare facility into a franchisee or by encouraging a new individual/group to set up a healthcare facility. The franchisee has the right to use a brand name and has to pay a fee for its use. In return, the franchisee gets a higher number of clients due to the brand name being popularised and benefits from technical support to ensure that his or her unit is viable. In a social franchisee arrangement, the objective is to offer a set of socially important services in the form of a franchisee operation. The private partner takes complete responsibility for marketing and distribution of low-cost health products (contraceptives, insecticidal bed nets, etc.).

14.7.8 Voucher Schemes: A voucher is a token or document which would ensure a specified range of services or goods for the user in place of cash. In this system the government defines the range of services (family planning services, delivery, transportation, caesarean delivery, ante-natal care, free medicines, etc.) which would be provided to the beneficiaries at fixed intervals based on criteria already defined by the government. It is a cashless transaction whereby the beneficiary gets the service without paying any money, while the government can target the subsidy to be provided and the private provider is reimbursed the cost based on actual outputs or performance.

These schemes cover the cost of deliveries of women with BPL cards in designated private hospitals. According to the scheme, the government pays the designated hospitals for each delivery and, in return, expects the hospital to provide vaginal or caesarean deliveries to the women with BPL cards free of cost and also cover a portion of travel costs.

14.7.9 Corporate Social Responsibility (CSR): The corporate sector partner or corporate associations, like the Confederation of Indian Industry (CII) and the Federation of Indian Chambers of Commerce and Industry (FICCI), provide support by way of funds and expertise in partnership with government. The CSR activities usually support development and health activities targeted at people living in areas near to their sites of operation.

15

Impediments and Challenges to PPP Model in India

India has witnessed considerable growth in PPPs in recent years and emerged as one of the leading PPP markets in the world. The PPP models being adopted by the Government are opening new avenues of investment and modernization. This will also bring in greater productivity and efficiency to the deployed capital.

PPPs across sectors in India are undergoing significant policy and regulatory reforms so as to reach the next level of maturity. The NITI Aayog, which has been mandated to provide directional and policy inputs to the Government, has deployed a federal cooperation structure to plan and execute some large PPP projects across states. This is truly an innovative approach toward building capacities at state government level.

Efforts of the Government are focused on a variety of issues, including rebalancing of risk sharing, renegotiation of contracts, need for an independent regulator, creation of a dispute resolution mechanism and strengthening of lending institutions. Efforts are being made by the Government to implement these recommendations.

Institutions such as the National Infrastructure Investment Fund (NIIF) are being promoted to provide financial stimulus to the sector. A Project Monitoring Group (PMG) has been created under Prime Minister's Office (PMO) to fast-track the approval process of large public and PPP projects. Further, the Government is in the process of making amendments in the Land Acquisition Act, 2013, Model Concession Agreements (MCAs), the Major Port Trusts Acts, 1963 etc. to streamline PPP regulatory frameworks.

Yet, PPP is a nascent concept in India, and expertise at the level of project authorities, both at the central and state levels, is limited. The awareness of concerns and issues relating to PPP is still lacking and not evenly spread across different States. To promote the PPP programme, all State Governments and Central Ministries have been advised to set up a PPP Cell with a senior level officer deputed as the PPP nodal officer.

Future development of infrastructure will depend on how investment in infrastructure is facilitated. Such investment requires long-term funds with long pay back periods, for example, from insurance and pension funds. Thus, success on the infrastructure front will be facilitated by the development of a vibrant bond market, and pension and insurance reforms. A single, unified exchange-traded market for corporate bonds would help create a mature debt market for financing infrastructure.

Impediments and challenges across the PPP lifecycle can be broadly classified into three categories:

1. Policy, legal, regulatory and institutional issues.
2. Financing issues and viability constraints.
3. Capacity and procedural challenges.

15.1 Policy, Legal, Regulatory and Institutional Issues

15.1.1 Absence of Dedicated PPP Policy at National Level: There is no PPP specific policy or law at national level. However, some State Governments have formulated laws and policies and set up the necessary institutional structures for streamlining PPPs, thereby formalizing the PPP landscape at a sub-national level. For example, the Government of Andhra Pradesh enacted The Andhra Pradesh Infrastructure Development Enabling Act, 2001 to provide for the rapid development of infrastructure and attract private sector participation in the state. Similarly, the Government of Gujarat enacted The Gujarat Infrastructure Development Act, 2006 in the state. Sector-specific acts or regulations and agencies for crucial sectors such as roads, airports, power, ports and railways exist at national level.

Some countries have a legal framework for PPPs in the form of PPP act/law/policy. A comprehensive national PPP act/policy which should clearly spell out the objectives, scope and implementing principles of the PPP programme envisaged by the Government is required to impart an authoritative framework to implementing executive agencies as well as to legislative and regulatory agencies charged with oversight responsibilities.

It may be relevant to mention that an attempt to formulate a National PPP Policy was made by the Department of Economic Affairs (DEA), Ministry of Finance in 2011 but it could not be concluded. Hence, there is a need to assess what went wrong in the process and whether we really need a Policy or Act to facilitate successful expansion of PPP in the country.

15.1.2 Judicial and Statutory Orders: A series of judicial and statutory authority orders (e.g. banning of mining activity) that delayed the progress of development and implementation of PPP projects and revenue flows. New projects are finding it increasingly difficult to attract sponsors, and financing (equity and debt) has become strained. Increased perceived risk of projects has further led to pension and insurance funds limiting their exposure to such projects.

Inadequate provisions to address legal and contractual issues (such as exit clauses provisions), default by parties, change of scope-related events, and connectivity infrastructure, have caused delays and projects not taking off as anticipated.

Implementing agencies often adopt model bidding and contract templates, with little or none of the project-specific customization that is key to successful project design and implementation.

Difficulties have been experienced with long-term PPP projects when parties are in dispute or unanticipated events lead to recourse to traditional long-drawn out legal systems for resolution.

15.1.3 Regulatory Framework: Sectors such as roads,

airports and ports have no independent regulator. Overlap in the functions of regulatory agencies has led to problems in certain cases, giving rise to calls for decisions taken at arm's length. Some sectors—such as the urban sector—are yet to evolve regulatory frameworks for sustainable and efficient delivery of PPP projects and services.

In airports sector, Airports Economic Regulatory Authority (AERA) was established by the government in 2009 as a statutory body under the Airports Economic Regulatory Authority of India Act, 2008 to act as an economic regulator of the airport infrastructure sector and air navigation services in the country.

15.1.4 Multiplicity of Institutions and Overlap in Roles: Governments at all levels, including urban local bodies (ULBs), line departments, state agencies, are by and large unable to create a steady pipeline of projects due to institutional capacity constraints. The network of multiple agencies involved in project implementation and an overlap in the functions of these agencies is leading to inordinate project delays. Agencies involved in PPP projects include NITI Aayog (erstwhile Planning Commission), Ministry of Finance, Department of Economic Affairs (DEA), various ministries, statutory entities like NHAI, AAI, and state governments. Effective co-ordination amongst various government agencies to deliver improved citizen value is cited as a key cause for delay of PPP projects. Inadequate capacity of authorities, consultants, financiers, developers, statutory audit and vigilance in the PPP context has given rise to misinformation. Lack of urban planning, and clear laws, regulations and procedures have resulted in a slowdown of urban infrastructure projects.

15.1.5 Dispute Resolution Mechanism: Due to the long-term nature of PPP contracts, uncertain market conditions, lack of capacity at both government and private player levels etc. disputes are bound to arise during the life cycle of PPP projects. Absence of regulators or multiplicity of regulators results in many of these issues and disputes being unresolved, leading to litigations and cases. This, in turn, leads to delays or cancellation of projects and results in cost escalation, thereby making the projects unviable.

Dispute resolution mechanisms are slow and not well-developed, often derailing project timelines and freezing funds. PPP projects have also been affected by factors such as delays in land acquisition and clearances, shifting of utilities, and right of way issues, leading to time and cost overruns.

According to the Chaturvedi Committee Report on the faster implementation of the National Highway Development Project (NHDP), an investment to the tune of ₹ 10,000 crore is held up in the NHDP alone, on account of the disputes between the National Highway Authority of India (NHAI) and the contractors.

While some states have developed framework and institutions in their states to fast-track the dispute resolution mechanism for PPP projects, there is absence of an efficient and credible dispute resolution mechanism at the national level. Various methods of alternative dispute resolution like amicable settlement, conciliation mediation, arbitration, expert adjudication, etc. are generally provided for in the concession contracts. However, these methods are proving to be inadequate for timely resolution of conflicts and issues in PPP projects.

15.2 Financing Issues and Viability Constraints.

15.2.1 Aggressive Bidding and Under-pricing of Projects: Aggressive bidding and under-pricing of projects have been a big challenge in the transport sector, particularly in roads and ports projects. Aggressive bidding is one of the major reasons for delays or cancellation of PPP project as banks are becoming more and more cautionary in funding such projects. It also causes low participation from genuine bidders.

Over-aggressive bidding with inadequate due diligence by bidders has sometimes led to unviable offers. Since determining whether a bidder's capital structuring permits such optimistic bidding is difficult for the public authorities. Bids are often accepted which later fail.

15.2.2 Inflated Total Project Cost (TPC) by the Bidders: It has been observed that some developers play opportunistically, facilitated by poor appraisal capacity of banks, by inflating the TPC and thereby achieving financial closure at an amount substantially greater than the reasonable TPC. If the project is then jeopardized, the funds at risk are those of the lenders as there is virtually no obligation on the developer.

The private sector has not developed its skills in pricing of risk, despite engaging the best consultants in the field. There is myopic assessment of possible risk factors and a failure to build in mitigation measures. Private sector developers, who are mainly construction experts, have no appetite for long-term operations and maintenance (O&M) of infrastructure assets. The country is yet to develop a specialist class of O&M developers who can take over during the operations phase. The quality of consultancy services in PPPs has not kept pace with the growing needs for such services in the country. This is reflected in inconsistent quality of some advisory services.

15.2.3 Huge Dependency on Commercial Banks for PPP Financing: Project sponsors in PPP projects depend hugely on commercial banks for financing the debt portion of the project. These banks have reached their corresponding exposure limits for the sector and run with high level of non-performing assets (NPAs) in the sector. Therefore, the infrastructure sector, in particular the transport sector, has been facing financing constraints of lately.

Bank appraisal of projects has, in many cases, suffered from lack of adequate diligence, sometimes due to inadequate appraisal skills. This has affected the quality of lending.

15.2.4 Over-leveraged Balance Sheet of Developers: The projects awarded are saturated among a few players. A variety of reasons including macroeconomic conditions, project delays and aggressive bidding have resulted in poor recovery from the projects, thereby making these companies over leveraged. This limits their capacity to raise funds from external sources and to take any more new projects.

Balance sheets of most prominent developers in the country are stressed and over leveraged. This festers twin balance sheet problem and results in inter-twined economic issues of over leveraged and distressed corporate and NPA encumbered banks.

15.2.5 Lack of Equity in the Market: Further, there is a shortfall in equity capital with local sponsors. Delays in execution of projects further lead to equity getting trapped in ongoing projects, thus not being available for newer projects. Underdeveloped debt markets have been a cause for concern for a while.

While there have been demands from developers for restructuring of existing contracts to sustain private sector interest, there is lack of appreciation of the sanctity of contracts and the need to restructure contracts that should be based on the project's revenues and long-term factors rather than temporary illiquidity and insolvency issues.

15.3 Capacity and Procedural Challenges

Many steps have been taken so far to address capacity and procedural challenges in the implementation of PPP projects. These steps include development of PPP approval mechanism, creation of autonomous bodies, launching of capacity building programs and publishing of guidelines, toolkits and MCAs. Despite these efforts, PPP projects in India face challenges such as lack of efficient project preparation activities, delay in land acquisition, delays in obtaining requisite approvals and clearances, and poor project monitoring activities. The capacity and procedural challenges in PPP projects are discussed below.

15.3.1 Lack of Efficient Project Preparation Activities: One of the most important steps in a PPP life cycle is the project preparation activities. Proper planning and preparation of projects improves the chances of success and smooth project implementation. Project preparation activities involve value for money (VfM) or public sector comparator (PSC) analysis, project structuring, risk assessment, and technical and financial due diligence. Other activities such as approvals and clearances can also form part of project preparation.

Despite the availability of an online toolkit on project preparation procedures, there is lack of capacities at various levels of government to properly plan and prepare PPP projects. Lack of capacities at various levels of the governments are evident in project preparation activities in many projects, resulting in problems such as cancellation or delay of project, arising of disputes and undue advantages to the private partner.

For undertaking PPP projects successfully, several factors continue to remain valid and intact—need for the project, appropriate project development, adequate project preparation, equitable risk allocation, transparent competitive procurement and an administrative, legal and regulatory ecosystem that promotes better value and services to the citizens and the public authorities, which result in better and cheaper long-term services.

Fundamental design flaws in PPP projects need to be tackled. For instance, contracts need to focus more on service delivery instead of fiscal benefits, better identification and allocation of risks between stakeholders, prudent utilization of VGF where user charges cannot guarantee a robust revenue stream, improved fiscal reporting practices and careful monitoring of performance.

It has been observed in many delayed and stalled projects, that the framework to assess project risks and allocate them between stakeholders has not been effectively developed. This has resulted in projects ending up in disputes, stretched project timelines and increased costs. Commercial and operational risks need to be passed on to the private sector under appropriate frameworks.

Most contracts in the PPP arena are under the construction and operations framework, while the need for model contracts for O&M and services is increasingly being perceived. There is a need to develop a new breed of O&M operators to take on projects that have been completed. The move to enable complete exit of promoters from the projects after a defined period, provides this flexibility.

15.3.2 Delay in Land Acquisition and/or Delay in Obtaining Approvals and Clearances: Infrastructure projects require multiple clearances at the centre, state and local levels, resulting in serious delays. The time taken to obtain all the requisite approvals for an infrastructure project can vary between a low of 18 months to as much as four to five years. Land acquisition and environmental clearance are the major contributing factors for project delays.

15.3.3 Inadequate and Inconclusive Stakeholder Consultations: It is important to consult and obtain buy-in of stakeholders to ensure the smooth implementation of projects, especially with regard to access, willingness to pay and dispute resolution. Going forward, it is possible to better manage the various risks that have plagued the Indian infrastructure sector with a more involved and participatory role of the private sector, and the allocation of risks in a manner that allows for flexibility to address concerns and reflect the interests of stakeholders. Such measures can also attract greater inflows of external debt and equity capital and thus lower the overall cost of capital for financing the infrastructural needs.

15.3.4 Inadequate Project Monitoring Activities: Project monitoring involves identification and enforcement of the concession agreement clauses during project implementation i.e. during construction and O&M period. Key activities include monitoring of the construction timeline, ensuring performance and safety standards, preventing misuse of assets, preventing any revenue or fund leakages, etc. While many activities are regularly monitored by the project authorities either directly or through an appointed agency, projects are not efficiently monitored on certain aspects like revenue safeguarding or fund management.

15.4 Slowdown of PPP Projects

The economic slowdown across the world and the credit crisis slowed the demand for goods and services across the spectrum, affecting the infrastructure sector significantly. The PPP projects were also impacted by this demand slowdown.

Macroeconomic developments in the late 2000s saw an overall slowdown in delivery and investment in infrastructure projects in general, including private sector projects and non-PPP projects, as in the case of the power sector. This, combined with country-specific issues—including weak capacity in public sector administration and private sector constraints to meet the requirements of a developing economy—led to a deleterious impact on investment in infrastructure, and choking of further capacity to invest by the private sector.

The recent slowdown of PPP projects could be attributed to a combination of events, namely global economic slowdown, weak regulatory and institutional frameworks, delay in issue of clearances by authorities, financing issues (over-leveraged debt and paucity of equity), aggressive bidding by developers, contractual issues (including long-drawn out dispute resolution), inadequate diligence and appraisal by lenders, and lack of flexibility in contractual arrangements. Coupled with parallel developments of increasing stress in non-PPP projects in major sectors such as power, the lending appetite to private sector and capacity for fresh infusion of funds became constrained, in both ongoing and new projects.

Further, though *transparency* in PPP projects is recognized as a crucial element for successful implementation of projects, (and projects pass through various stages and are configured based on complex policies and programmes), there are increasing demands from the private sector for a review of the *rigidity* in model concession documents and rebalancing of risks. While recognizing that government faces a moral hazard in allowing post-award change in contracts, the DEA undertook a study to address this issue, and also the need to institutionalize long-term contract management processes by public authorities.

Apart from public implementing authorities, some stakeholders have pointed towards the possibility of opportunistic gaming by developers in the bidding process, facilitated by inadequate appraisal by lenders. By inflating the total project cost (TPC), developers achieve financial closure at an amount substantially greater than reasonable TPC and thereby source higher debt than the actual requirement. If the project is then jeopardized, the funds at risk are those of the lenders as there is virtually no *skin in the game* by the developer.

15.5 Public-Private-Partnership: A Critique

There have been a number of critics associated with PPP in India, in particular related to the risks that come with such partnerships.

It has been argued that PPP involve greater costs that traditional government procurement processes (because of the development, bidding and ongoing costs in PPP projects). Some have questioned the value-for-money relevance of PPP projects in India.

The private sector does not provide a service that is not specifically outlined in the PPP contract. It is thus critical that key performance indicators are precisely laid out in the contract and that the government monitors closely the work of its private partner.

Furthermore, there is a cost attached to debt and while private sector can help access to finance, it the customers or the government may end up bearing much of this cost.

Another criticism of PPP projects is related to their social and political consequences, which can be significant. For example, a PPP project may result in the transfer of civil servants to the private sector, important tariff increases or resettlement issues to name a few.

PPPs often end up being renegotiated. This is due to the long-term nature of the PPP projects (some run for up to 30 years) and their complexity. It is difficult to identify all possible contingencies during project development and events and issues may arise that were not anticipated in the documents or by the parties at the time of the contract.

Other major drawbacks encountered in 3P projects in India include poorly drafted contracts and lack of understanding of contracts, inadequate resources, lack of managerial experience, breaches of contract, failures in team building, lack of performance measures, corruption and political interference.

Appendix

Appendix

Report of the Committee on Revisiting and Revitalising the PPP Model of Infrastructure Development, 2015

Highlights and Recommendations

In his Budget Speech to the Parliament, while presenting the Budget for the year 2015-16, the Finance Minister Shri Arun Jaitley had announced that the PPP mode of infrastructure development has to be revisited and revitalised. In pursuance of this announcement, a Committee on Revisiting and Revitalising the PPP Model of Infrastructure Development was set up under the chairmanship of Dr. Vijay Kelkar. The Committee submitted its report to the Finance Ministry on November 19, 2015.

Terms of Reference

The Committee was constituted with the following terms of reference:

1. Reviewing the experience of PPP policy, including the variations in contracts and the difficulties experienced.
2. Analysing the risks involved in PPP projects in different sectors and the framework of risk sharing between the project developer and the government.
3. Proposing design modifications to the contractual arrangements of PPPs based on the above.
4. Proposing measures to improve capacity building in government for effective implementation of PPP projects.

Highlights of the Report

1. PPPs in infrastructure represent a valuable instrument to speed up infrastructure development in India. This

speeding up is urgently required for India to grow rapidly and generate a demographic dividend for itself and also to tap into the large pool of pension and institutional funds from aging populations in the developed countries.

2. India offers today the world's largest market for PPPs. It has accumulated a wealth of experience in getting to this premiere position. As the PPP market in infrastructure matures in India, new challenges and opportunities have emerged and will continue to emerge. Periodic review of PPPs are a must to help address issues before they become endemic and to mainstream innovations and foster new ones that improve the successful delivery of PPP projects.
3. India's success in deploying PPPs as an important instrument for creating infrastructure in India will depend on a change in attitude and in the mind-set of all authorities dealing with PPPs, including public agencies partnering with the private sector, government departments supervising PPPs, and auditing and legislative institutions providing oversight of PPPs.
4. Measures may be taken immediately to make only malafide action by public servants punishable, and not errors, and to guard against witch hunt against government officers and bureaucrats for decisions taken with bonafide intention. The government may speed up amendment of the Prevention of Corruption Act, 1988 and Vigilance and Conduct rules applicable to government officers.
5. Experience has also underlined the need to further strengthen the three key pillars of PPP frameworks, namely governance, institutions and capacity, to build on the established foundation for the next wave of implementation.
6. In addition to changing mind-sets, there is an urgent need to rebuild India's PPP capacities. Structured capacity building programmes for different stakeholders including implementing agencies and customized programmes for banks and financial institutions and private sector need to be evolved. The need for a national level institution to support

institutional capacity building activities must be explored. Every stakeholder without exception has strongly emphasised the urgent need for a dedicated institute for PPPs as was announced in the previous Budget.

7. The Committee cannot overstate the criticality of setting up of independent regulators in sectors that are going in for PPPs. The Committee recommends setting up these independent regulators with a unified mandate that encompasses activities in different infrastructure sub-sectors to ensure harmonized performance by the regulators.
8. The Committee welcomes the current review and amendment of the Arbitration Act, and strongly endorses the need for time limits on hearings.
9. The dominant, primary concern of the Committee was the optimal allocation of risks across PPP stakeholders. Inefficient and inequitable allocation of risk in PPPs can be a major factor in PPP failures, ultimately hurting the citizens of India. The Committee notes that the adoption of the Model Concession Agreement (MCA) has meant that project specific risks are rarely addressed by project implementation authorities in this *one-size-fits-all* approach. A rational allocation of risks can only be undertaken in sector and project-specific contexts.
10. For the next generation of PPP contracts, the Committee suggests the following broad guidelines while allocating and managing risks:

- An entity should bear the risk that is in its normal course of its business.
- An assessment needs to be carried out regarding the relative ease and efficiency of managing the risk by the entity concerned.
- The cost effectiveness of managing the risk needs to be evaluated.
- Any overriding considerations/stipulations of a particular entity need to be factored in prior to implementing the risk management structure.

11. Typically infrastructure PPP projects span over 20-30 years and a developer often loses bargaining power related to tariffs and other matters in case there are abrupt changes in the economic or policy environment which is beyond his control. The Committee feels strongly that the private sector must be protected against what have been called "Obsolescing Bargain"—the loss of bargaining power over time by private player in PPPs—through mechanisms including the setting up of independent sector regulators.
12. PPP projects can become distressed when risks emerge that may not have been contemplated at the time of signing. This could give rise to a call for amending the terms of the Concession Agreement to reflect new project realities better. The Committee has suggested benchmarks to be applied to each proposed renegotiation as well as set out a set of conditions that should not be accepted as valid reasons for a request for amendment of a concession agreement.
13. The final decision on a renegotiated concession agreement must be based on:

- Full disclosure of the renegotiated estimated long-term costs, risks and potential benefits.
- Comparison with the financial position for government at the time of signing the concession agreement.
- Comparison with the existing financial position for government just prior to renegotiation. This will permit the authority regulating the concession to take a decision based on a full comparison of the likely outcomes over the future of the concession.

14. The Committee recognizes the need for a quick, equitable, efficient and enforceable dispute resolution mechanism for PPP projects. It is suggested that PPP contracts have clearly articulated dispute resolution structures that demonstrate commitment of all stakeholders and provide flexibility to restructure within the commercial and financial boundaries of the project.
15. The authorities may be advised against adopting PPP

structures for very small projects, since the benefits of delivering small PPP projects may not be commensurate with the resulting costs and the complexity of managing such partnerships over a long period. The transaction costs of well-structured PPP projects are significant, including essential but expensive expert advisory services.

16. Unsolicited proposals ("Swiss Challenge") may be actively discouraged as they bring information asymmetries into the procurement process and result in lack of transparency and fair and equal treatment of potential bidders in the procurement process.
17. Inherent in the concept of PPP is the role of a "private sector partner" that will implement the project, based on the need to leverage private sector financing and also the managerial and operational efficiencies of the private sector party. It is in this context that the Committee is of the view that since state owned entities SoEs/PSUs are essentially Government entities and work within the government framework, they should not be allowed to bid for PPP projects.
18. The authorities should not treat PPPs as an off-balance sheet funding method for the government's responsibility of providing reliable infrastructure services to its citizens. PPPs should not be used as the first delivery mechanism without checking its suitability for a particular project. States and other agencies should also not treat Central PPP VGF as a source of additional grants that can be accessed by adopting a PPP delivery mode for projects that are not suitable for such a long-term financing structure.
19. There have been concerns raised by all stakeholders (Government and Private Sector alike) on the demand for developer books of account being subjected to government audit and for access under RTI and Article 12 of the Constitution. Conventional audit by authority of private partner's books as per standard procurement process risks delivery of poor quality of service/public asset provision if

there is no certainty of processes in the medium-term. To address this, the Committee recommends that the government notify comprehensive guidelines on the applicability and scope of such activities. The laid down process would enable review only of government internal systems, and not that of SPVs but SPVs would need to follow best practice in corporate governance systems including those related to related party transactions, financial disclosures etc. as in the Companies Act, 2013.

20. Equity in completed, successful infrastructure projects may be divested by offering to long-term investors, including overseas institutional investors as domestic and foreign institutional investors with long-term liabilities are best suited for providing such long-term financing, but have a limited appetite for risk. Cash generated out of divestment of equity would be available for the creation of new infrastructure projects in the country
21. It is necessary to explore options for sourcing long term capital at low cost. Towards this, the Committee recommends, encouraging the banks and financial institution to issue deep discount bonds or zero coupon bonds (ZCB). These will not only lower debt servicing costs in an initial phase of project but also enable the authorities to charge lower user charges in initial years.
22. Some countries have a legal framework for PPPs in the form of PPP Act/Law/Policy. Ministry of Finance may develop and publish a national PPP Policy document. Ideally, such a policy document should be endorsed by the Parliament as a policy resolution to impart an authoritative framework to implementing executive agencies as well as to legislative and regulatory agencies charged with oversight responsibilities. The Committee recommends an assessment of whether formulating and enacting a PPP law will facilitate successful expansion of PPP into new sectors, including health, other social sectors, and urban transport.
23. In the final analysis, the success of deploying PPP as an

additional policy instrument for creating infrastructure in India will depend on the change in attitudes and mindsets of all the authorities including public agencies partnering the private sector, government departments supervising the PPPs, and auditing and legislative institutions providing oversight of the PPPs. The PPP reflects a paradigm shift involving the private sector. It means moving away from "transaction to relationship", accommodating "give and take" between private and public sector partners, and finally accepting uncertainties and appropriate adjustments inherent in implementing long-time contracts. The Committee urges all parties concerned to foster trust between the private sector and public sector partners in implementing PPP.

Main Recommendations

I. Revisiting PPPs: Achievements and Challenges

1. Contracts need to focus more on service delivery instead of fiscal benefits.
2. Better identification and allocation of risks between stakeholders.
3. Prudent utilization of viability gap funds where user charges cannot guarantee a robust revenue stream.
4. Improved fiscal reporting practices and careful monitoring of performance a. Given the urgency of India's demographic transition, and the experience India has already gathered in managing PPPs, the government must move the PPP model to the next level of maturity and sophistication.

II. Why it is Urgent for India to Get Infrastructure PPPs?

1. Given the urgency of India's demographic transition, and the experience India has already gathered in managing PPPs, the government must move the PPP model to the next level of maturity and sophistication.
2. The Committee feels strongly that maturing the PPP model in India is an urgent priority also to take advantage of this

historical conjunction of India's infrastructure needs and the availability of long-term funding.

3. PPPs have the potential to deliver infrastructure projects both faster and better. Building on India's 15 years of experience with PPPs, there is a need to iron out the difficulties in the performance of PPP at every stage of the contract.

III. Re-balancing of Risk Sharing

1. An assessment needs to be carried out regarding the relative ease and efficiency of managing the risks by the entity concerned.
2. Cost effectiveness of managing the risk needs to be evaluated.
3. Sophisticated modelling techniques are prevalent to assess probabilities of risks and the need to provision for them. Department of Economic Affairs (DEA), Ministry of Finance may hone its skills in this and provide guidance to project authorities.
4. The final decision for a renegotiated Concession Agreement must be based on.

- Full disclosure of long-term costs, risks and potential benefits.
- Comparison with the financial position for government at the time of signing the Concession Agreement.
- Comparison with the financial position for government at the time prior to renegotiation.

IV. Resolving Legacy Issues

1. Only a statutorily established credible empowered multi-disciplinary expert institutional mechanism can deal with the complex issues involved:

- An Infrastructure PPP Project Review Committee (IPRC) may be constituted to evaluate and send its recommendations in a time-bound manner upon a reference being made of actionable stress in any infrastructure project developed in PPP mode beyond a notified threshold value.

- An Infrastructure PPP Adjudication Tribunal (IPAT) chaired by a Judicial Member (former Judge SC/Chief Justice HC) with a technical and/or a financial member, where benches will be constituted by the chairperson as per needs of the matter in question.

2. In case procurement of land or clearance is pending from government authorities for more than prescribed number of days, the outstanding work should be descoped (under the provisions of Change in Law of Concession Agreement), and allow rest of activities for completed work. Balance work could be completed on a cash-contract basis, provided land and required clearances are in place.
3. Cancel projects that have not achieved a prescribed percentage of progress on the ground. Rebid them once issues have been resolved or complete them through public funds and if viable, bid out for operations and maintenance.

V. Generic, Including Legacy Projects

1. Sector specific institutional frameworks may be developed to address issues for PPP infrastructure projects. An entity should bear the risk that is in its normal course of its business (for instance, acquisition of land is a normal course of business for public entities). Overriding considerations/stipulations of each entity to be factored in prior to implementation of risk management structure.
2. Learnings from the highways sector to be utilized for other sectors to customize and adopt such frameworks.
3. Umbrella guidelines may be developed for stressed projects that provide an overall framework for development and functioning of the sector specific frameworks.
4. DEA to finalize a national PPP Policy document.
5. Unsolicited proposals (Swiss Challenge) to be discouraged to avoid information asymmetries and lack of transparency.
6. PPP structures not to be adopted for very small projects in view of the transaction costs involved. DEA to issue a threshold guidance.

VI. Strengthening Policy, Governance and Institutional Capacity

1. Amend the Prevention of Corruption Act, 1988 to distinguish between genuine errors in decision-making and acts of corruption.
2. Build up capacity in all stakeholders, including regulators, authority, consultants, financing agencies, developers.
3. Set up an institution for invigorating private investments in infrastructure, providing guidance for a national PPP policy and developments in PPP, developing a mechanism to capture and collate data for decision-making, undertaking capacity building activities.
4. Pre-qualified PPP consultancies could be empanelled by DEA as earlier which could be tapped at short notice.
5. Revive the PPP Cells supported by the DEA over the last decade in Infrastructure Ministries and State Governments.
6. An institutionalized mechanism like the National Facilitation Committee (NFC) to ensure time bound resolution of issues including getting timely clearances and approvals during implementation of projects for smooth running of such projects.
7. Ministry of Finance to coordinate with other implementing ministries may develop a policy to promote secondary market for operational assets.
8. Disallow statutory audit to books of SPVs governed by the provisions of the Companies Act. Ensure adoption of principles of good governance by the SPVs
9. Standard public authority requirements of audit till point of award (public books) and post-construction discharge by Authority of monitoring and oversight of project operations as per the concession agreement (public books) to be in the purview of statutory/government audit agencies.
10. Essential to set up independent regulators in sectors going in for PPP.
11. Discourage government participation in SPVs that implement PPP projects unless strategically essential.

VII. Scaling-up Finance

1. Restrict the number of banks in a consortium.
2. Banks to build up their own risk assessment/appraisal capabilities.
3. Check list of items listed as a guidance for lenders.
4. RBI may provide guidelines to lenders on encashment of bank guarantees in line with ICC norms.
5. Monetisation of viable projects that have stable revenue flows after EPC delivery should be considered.
6. Equity in completed, successful infrastructure projects may be divested by offering to long-term investors.
7. Ministry of Finance to allow banks and financial institutions to issue Zero Coupon Bonds which will also help to achieve soft landing for user charges in infrastructure sector.

VIII. Revitalising Contractual Processes

1. Need for review of the MCAs.
2. Sample suggestions for generic changes, including for resolution of disputes, and sector-specific changes.

IX. Reinvigorating the Sectors

1. Independent sector regulators essential.
2. Build upon maturing landscape in roads and ports PPP and move into the next phase.

- Roads: Avoiding delays, institutionalized dispute resolution, improved project development activity, monetization of operational assets, efficiency and transparency by electronic tolling etc.
- Ports: Review of role and need of Tariff Authority for Major Ports (TAMP), review of MCA, quicker clearances, rationalized leases and stamp duties.
- Airport: PPPs to be encouraged where viable in greenfield and brownfield projects, have policy that addresses potential demand for airport services in the country, notify a unified regulatory structure.

3. Encourage use of PPPs in sectors like Railways, Urban, etc. Railways to have an independent tariff regulator, tap potentially useful PPP opportunities including brownfield assets.

X. Fast Forward PPPs

1. Set up an institute of excellence in PPP to inter alia guide the sector, provide policy input, timely advice and undertake sustainable capacity building.
2. Ensure integrated development of infrastructure with roadmaps for delivery of projects.
3. India's demographic deadlines are staring at us. There are only two or three decades left to complete the transition from a country that has just attained middle-income status to that of a high-income and developed economy. Besides the basic problems for provision of adequate infrastructure, the middle-income trap is also to be averted. Without adequate infrastructure, this will simply not be possible. India is currently in a global win-win situation with a large young population that will need good jobs and a huge pool of global savings that can be tapped for building out our infrastructure. PPPs are an important policy instrument that will enable India to compress time in this journey towards economic growth and development. A successful and growing stream of PPPs in infrastructure will go a long way in accelerating the country's development process.

Bibliography

Bibliography

Ahluwalia, Montek S. (1998), "Infrastructure Development in India's Reforms", in 'India's Economic Reforms and Development: Essays for Manmohan Singh', Isher J. Ahluwalia and IMD Little (eds.), Oxford University Press, New Delhi.

Anand, Y.P. (1998), "Reforming Indian Railways Financial Management' in 'Indian Railway Finance', K.B. Verma (ed.), Academic Foundation, New Delhi.

Bellier, Michel, and Yue Maggie Zhou (2003), "Private Participation in Infrastructure in China: Issues and Recommendations for the Road, Water, and Power Sectors", World Bank Working Paper No. 2, Washington, D.C.

Chandavarkar, A. (1995), "Infrastructure Finance; Issues, Institution and Policies", World Bank Policy Research Working Paper No. 1374.

Dalvi, M.Q. and S. Sriraman (1998), "Indian Railway Tariff Policy", *Indian Economic Journal*, October-December.

David, Newbery M. (2000), "Privatization, Restructuring, and Regulation of Network Utilities", MIT Press, Cambridge, Massachusetts.

Deaton, A. and Jean Dreze (2002), "Poverty and Inequality in India: A Re-examination", *Economic and Political Weekly*, September 7.

Dholakia, R.H. and D. Kapur (2001), "Economic Reforms and Trade Performance: Private Corporate Sector in India", *Economic and Political Weekly,* Volume 36, No. 49, December.

Dreze, Jean and A. Sen (2002), "India: Development and Participation", Oxford University Press, New Delhi.

ESCAP (1994), "Infrastructure Development as Key to Economic Growth and Regional Economic Cooperation", United Nations.

ESCAP (1997), "Mobilising Private Sector Resources for Infrastructure", United Nations.

European Commission (2003), "Guidelines for Successful Public-Private-Partnerships", Brussels, March.

Government of India, *Economic Survey* (various years).

——*Industrial Policy Statement, 1991.*

——Ministry of Finance, *Budget Speech of the Finance Minister* (various years).

——Ministry of Law, Justice and Company Affairs, *Constitution of India.*

——Report of the Committee on Transport Policy and Coordination, Planning Commission, 1966.

——Status Paper on Indian Railways: Issues and Options, Ministry of Railways, 1998.

——Ministry of Finance, Department of Economic Affairs, *Report of the Committee on Revisiting and Revitalising Public Private Partnership Model of Infrastructure*, November 2015.

Gupta, D.P. (1999), "Modernising Road Infrastructure", paper presented at National Seminar on Road and Road Transport Policy, Indian Merchants Chamber, Mumbai.

Harris, Clive (2003), "Private Participation in Infrastructure in Developing Countries: Trends, Impacts, and Policy Lessons", World Bank Working Paper No. 5. Washington D.C.

Harris, Clive, John Hodges, Michael Schur and Padmesh Shukla (2003), "Infrastructure Projects: A Review of Canceled Private Projects", Public Policy for the Private Sector Note No. 252, January, Washington D.C.

Kapur, A. (1995), "Airport Infrastructure: Emerging Role of the Private Sector", World Bank Technical Paper No. 313.

Kesavan, K.V. (ed.) (2001), "Economic Liberalization in India: Japanese and Indian Perspectives", Indian Council of Social Science Research, Manak Publications, New Delhi.

Krishna, P. and D. Mitra (1998), "Trade Liberalisation, Market Discipline and Productivity Growth: New Evidence from India", *Journal of Development Economics*, August.

Krishnaswamy, V. and Gary Stuggins (2001), "Private Sector Participation in the Power Sector in ECA Countries: Lessons Learned from the Last Decade", Technical Paper, Washington D.C.

Kumar, Sasi and C. Jayasankar Prasad (2004), "Public-Private-Partnerships in Urban Infrastructure", *Kerala Calling*, February.

Malini, E. (1997), "Evaluation of Financial Viability of BOT Transport Infrastructure Projects", *Journal of India Road Congress.*

Mody, A (1997), "Infrastructure Strategies in East Asia", World Bank Economic Development Institute, Learning Resources Series.

Mody, A. (ed.) (1996), "Infrastructure Delivery and the Public Good", World Bank, Washington D.C.

Nasir, Tyabji (2000), "Industrialisation and Innovation: The Indian Experience", Sage Publications, New Delhi.

Queiroz, Cesar (2005), "Launching Public-Private-Partnerships for Highways in Transition Economies", World Bank Transport Papers No. 9, September, Washington D.C.

Quiggin, John (2004), "Risks, PPPs and the Public Sector Comparator", *Australian Accounting Review*, 14(2): 51-62.

Rajaraman, Indira (2005), "Financing Rural Infrastructure in Developing Countries", *Applied Econometrics and International Development*, Volume 5.

Rajasekhar, D. (2000), "Non-government Organizations (NGOs) in India: Opportunities and Challenges", *Journal of Rural Development*, Volume 19, No. 2.

Ramamurti, Ravi (1996), "The New Frontier of Privatization", in R. Ramamurti (ed.), 'Privatizing Monopolies: Lessons from the Telecommunications and Transport Sectors in Latin America', John Hopkins University Press, Baltimore, Maryland.

Razib, Ahmed (2006), "Infrastructure Development: India's Biggest Challenge", *Know More India*, August 6.

Rivera, Daniel (1996), "Private Sector Participation in the Water Supply and Wastewater Sector: Lessons from Six Developing Countries", World Bank, Washington D.C.

Sriraman, S. (1998), "Report of the Sub-Committee on Financing Taxation, Pricing and Insurance of Trucking Sector in India", submitted to the Steering Committee on Trucking Industry in India, Ministry of Surface Transport, Government of India.

Sriraman, S. (2000), "Indian Railway Finances: Critical Issues and Emerging Options", *Economic and Political Weekly*, Volume 35, March.

Sriraman, S. and A. Bagchi (1997), "Financing Transport Infrastructure and Services in India", *Asian Transport Journal*, May.

Swaroop, V. (1996), "Public Finance of Infrastructure: Issues and Options", in A. Mody, (ed.), 'Infrastructure Delivery and the Public Good', World Bank, Washington D.C.

UNCTAD, *Trade and Development Report* (various issues).

United Nations Industrial Development Organization (UNIDO) (1996), "Guidelines for Infrastructure Development through

Build-Operate-Transfer (BOT) Projects", UNIDO, New York.

World Bank (2001), "New Designs for Water and Sanitation Transactions: Making Private Sector Participation Work for the Poor", Washington D.C.

——(1994), "Infrastructure for Development", *World Development Report*.

——*World Development Report* (various years).

——*(1997),* "Private Sector in Infrastructure: Strategy, Regulation and Risk".

Yamazawa, Ippei (2000), "Developing Economies in the Twenty-First Century: The Challenge of Globalisation", Institute of Developing Economies, Japan.

Websites

Ministry of Commerce and Industry
Ministry of Heavy Industries and Public Enterprises
Ministry of Railways
Ministry of Road Transport and Highways
Ministry of Shipping
Ministry of Civil Aviation
Ministry of Electronics and Information Technology
Ministry of Information and Broadcasting
Ministry of Power
Ministry of Petroleum and Natural Gas
Ministry of Urban Development
Ministry of Rural Development
Ministry of Housing and Urban Affairs
Ministry of Finance
NITI Aayog
Reserve Bank of India

Index

Index